'Parents, Teachers, and Governors, I Am Afraid to Tell You…'

by Vivica Houston

RoseDog❖Books
PITTSBURGH, PENNSYLVANIA 15238

RoseDog Books
585 Alpha Drive
Suite 103
Pittsburgh, PA 15238
Visit our website at *www.rosedogbookstore.com*

ISBN: 978-1-6470-2100-9
eISBN: 978-1-6470-2076-7

CONTENTS

INTRODUCTION

Here is the generation where virginity is despised and virgins become promiscuous in order to fit in. Here is the generation that forbids marriage, that dishonors parents, heritage, legacy, Family Crests and family businesses. Here is the generation of self-imposed disfigurement to fit an imaginary model of beauty: skin burning, skin bleaching, shaved-scalp hair-dos, body part enhancements, arm-sleeves and torso tattoos, bizarre face piercings, skin paint, ear clipping, etc.

We have created a new normal that involves not getting married to the one you love while you are a virgin. A new normal in which people in the Land of the Free do not make their own decisions and choose to follow their own path when they are finished with being called a child. We have a new normal of forced childhood, by rule of law. Over-protecting, over-parenting, over-indulging and over-pampering a group of people who do not contribute to the economy because of the rule of law.

What would teenagers do if the brakes were taken off? How would teenagers conduct themselves given full freedom to make big decisions and learn life-affirming skills to better their situations? If from the age of 13 a young person could be considered equal to the 18 year old, would that young person have more hope and energy to study harder and work harder to get out of poverty, immorality and criminal activities? Would that young person take voting rights seriously? Would that young person take liberation and emancipation soberly enough to make the best decisions that they can to keep family and lifestyle under control, in order to work a legitimate job and stay out of trouble with law enforcement?

CHAPTER ONE

13 YEARS IS LONG ENOUGH TO BE A CHILD

"Rejoice, young man, in your youngness and let your heart cheer you in the days of your youth, and walk in the ways of your heart and in the sight of your eyes...for childhood and youth are vanity." Ecclesiastes 11:9

We need 13 year olds to be given freedom to just say "NO!" to further junk food education and forced learning. Let them choose to be human over being robots. Give them rights to marry who they love and rights to work full time jobs and take over their own God-ordained destiny and personal lives. Support them emotionally and financially whenever necessary. Allow them to drive cars, sign leases and buy homes according to their maturity and intelligence. All 18 year olds are not smarter than every 13 year old. Adult-hood is not a magic number.

This government has too much power over our lives, deciding if we are old enough to work a job and live without parental supervision. When is our country going to stop trying to control and manipulate people? When will people be really allowed to decide for themselves if they want to remain children, or if they want to keep going to school after the 8th grade? Eight years minimum is a very long time already, then four more, then another four years minimum for college, when do we begin to live? When do we sit at home with our parents and just be human beings before we turn 18? When do we take a break from being human encyclopedias? This government has too much power over our lives deciding if we are old enough to work a job and live without parental supervision at the beginning of our teen years.

Just like kids who turn 18 have a choice to keep being mom and dad's little baby until they get ready to get out into the world, I want that kind of choice for 13 year olds because of the mental suffering that I myself went through. Poor kids want their parents' love and approval so they are not very likely to take advantage of legal rights to become an Emancipated Teenager. This is also controlling poor people, especially Black Americans, from reproducing. We are the number one group aborting babies or saving ourselves for marriage in our teens. We are also controlling ourselves from falling in love. No one is getting married in their teens anymore. So we have the guilt and shame of children born outside of marriage. The rage and anger that comes from a forced education with an irrelevant curriculum should not be in control of our children's lives and futures. We are human beings, we are not data consuming robots.

This culture needs to allow children the right to choose childhood if they are immature and irresponsible; or adulthood if they are mature and responsible at the age of 13. This system needs to minimize the education bubble and expand the family and friendship bubble. At the end of our lives families and friendships matter a lot more than academic scholarships and college diplomas. With the rise in gun crimes a lot of young people in America are residing in Heaven by the age of 18. In view of the worst case scenario a teen pregnancy or teen marriage is not a bad choice after all. How sad to go to the shooting gallery called high school for 4 years without experiencing love or parenthood.

Oh of course there are the run-away child tragedies. Due to the juvenile delinquents who will not conform to anyone's laws but their own. Just like truant officers were excessive policing, the legal age law is also excessive policing. When a 13 year old does a crime that took maturity and planning to accomplish, guess what? He or she will be declared an adult through the court system. It was not spontaneous or impulsive, but it was a planned crime in which the underage person was counting on the system to try him or her as a juvenile. Had they been considered a legal adult in the first place, they would not have committed the crime. The good kids admire them while afraid of getting into trouble. A child who lives in the eye of trouble no matter what, quits trying to toe that line. Yet his or her effort to survive is all against the law because they are 13 years old or under 18. They are not supposed to work a legitimate job full time. They are not supposed to be driving a car. They are not supposed to be living on their own alone in an apartment or house. They are not supposed to be romantically involved with someone over 18, or that person will likely do prison time and register as a sex offender if turned in.

Law has become God. How is that a good thing? Does this present atmosphere in 21st Century North America of random homicides, patricides, infanticides and suicides, look like a dream? Or isn't this really a nightmare? Help America be a nation of heroes, happy families and good neighbors again. Crime sprees are not isolated to poor suburbs, it is already spilling out into affluent suburbs as you read this book.

The Greatest Generation that grew up during the Great Depression did not have mandatory high school and blind ambition telling them how to live their lives. As soon as they felt confident, sometimes while still preparing, they were thrust out into the working world. Instead of high school with its cheer leaders, sports and dances, they worked full-time jobs without benefits. They walked the 5 miles to work and transportation problems were never an excuse for not maintaining a legitimate job. Being 13 years old was not an excuse for not helping your parents pay the rent.

Allowing 13 year olds emancipation or adulthood, will help them survive poverty and reversals of fortune. Legal age does not mean parents are no longer necessary. Whatever age we are, we are always our parents babies. Legal age is not even in the Bible. We have made life too complicated for our own good. We are overly concerned about education and getting a job. The problem with that is, opportunity to make it rich can arrive on the scene at 13 and disappear at 18. Especially for young people who are gifted at sports, art, music, writing, dancing, acting, modeling, public speaking and journalism. Love can arrive on the scene at 13 and disappear at 18, forever.

Thirteen is a magic age for so many young people. An age of self-control and respect for authority, of moral virtues and faith in God with beautiful ideas and inventions. This is an age to be tapped into for greatness. We keep wanting adulthood to have a number. There are lots of 18-year old babies. Adulthood might be the ability to clean your house, get your body out of the bed on time to go to a daily job and say "no" to crime with no one watching over you and know when to call for help, plain and simple, no matter what your chronological age is. Adulthood is also continuing personal education, living on a budget, setting financial savings goals, religious connections, giving to charity and community improvement programs, looking after younger siblings and being of service to one's family first. Also, knowing that if you are not ready to mate, then you do not need to date. If you agree with me, even a little bit, look at your child. Look at your child as capable of taking care of the business of living on their own. Maybe that young person can skip public high-school and go directly to a community college or a full time job.

Parents of rebellious teens need a way out and their teens need life-affirming legalized choices. If, 13 became an age in which one could live on one's own and get a job without being labeled a delinquent, that would be a step in the right direction. Having 13 as a legal emancipation age can help parents who are disabled by drug addiction or mental illness. Young people can rise to the challenges of poverty and parental dysfunction by taking care of younger siblings, working a full time job, paying the rent and buying food without the fear of child protection services breaking up their family.

CPS could be a support system as long as the young people are cooperative and law abiding. CPS could make sure they have enough food to eat, bus passes and clothing. In this high tech generation there are far more advantages than disadvantages. We have too many human beings to be holding back a group of people who could help lift their parents up out of the poverty zone. There are still poor families that I know of, in the Black community, who have never had a parent own a car, or learn how to drive. Who experience generational poverty, no matter that all of their children and grandchildren graduated from high school. This is not a good picture.

We would be better parents and teachers if we were given only 13 years to get the job done. We would have no problem teaching moral values and life skills. Would it drive down the crime rate? Would it heighten respect for law enforcement and authority figures? Would it help the poor people who have never had a generation of prosperity rise up enough to eat a plate of fried calamari and pickled caviar? Would it make it easier for the courts when a 13 year-old commits an adult crime? That would be nice, but what is at issue here is the charge of Child Abuse.

America, how are you? I hereby charge you, my beloved country, with child abuse under the heading of public education. You have been using the public school system to abuse children and cheat them out of their relationships with an all knowing God since I was born. A God who knows better than a government law who is ready for adulthood and raising children, running a household, driving a car and working jobs. A God who will not work you into an early grave or into a mental illness trying to maintain a GPA of 4.0 in the name of "The American Dream." Five years can feel like ten. Adults seem to be numb to the stress of trying to maintain a child-like image as a teenager.

In this century we have so much more knowledge as a modernized country; with so many inventions and so many laws in place that will protect young workers from unfair treatment and sexual exploitation. As we enter the 22nd Century we can no longer afford to keep our children babies for 18 years. Our system is greatly flawed and extremely behind its own schedule. How do we look at science fiction films or read books on the future and still start first grade at 6 years old? Our children deserve to be challenged in the educational system, or what is the point?

A two year old can learn how to read "Dick and Jane," just give them the chance. America, my book is a "wake-up call" to you. People are dying in so many unexpected ways, we cannot afford to have able-bodied people who can work jobs sitting around the house watching TV and reading books all day, by rule of law. All hands need to be on the deck, America. Our sons and our daughters need to be on their own, alone in an apartment or house. They are supposed to be ready and willing to defend our country through military service, or support their parents working full time jobs until their branch of the family tree rises out of poverty.

It is time to change this culture of giving babies away (or erasing them) as a solution to a problem of unreadiness and financial distress. It is time to give teens the tools they need to be successful instead of always believing that they are going to fail. Our country needs to help teenagers become competent and ready for whatever life will throw at them.

The poor places of America would benefit from legally allowing mature and disciplined 13 year olds to take control of their living situations. The sooner we get our young people on the ground and running, the better for the system. We have too many depressed people, too many anti-social people who are smart with college degrees, but do not have social, family or work skills. The public school system needs to weed out the ones who can make it at the youngest age they can. So they can support themselves and begin learning how to manage their lives without all the baggage. Under 18, adults are there for you, at 18, people are done with you. They start looking at you like you are stupid for not knowing what you should know about everyday life.

Like the TV show, <u>THE PRETENDER</u>, the principle character, Jared, had never seen a "Twinkie" before or tasted ice cream and people looked at him sideways. On a TV show it might be a little amusing, but in real life it is awful to turn 18 years old and not even know what a money order is or a debit card. Here you are, considered an adult, but you have never before cashed a check or opened a bank account. Running around clueless about everyday life and getting angry at not knowing how the systems for living on your own operate—18 years is simply too old for that. At 13 you will have a lot more sympathy and a lot more helpers to become a skilled and knowledgeable adult. Not implying anything about sexual relations, there is more to adulthood than sexual competency.

Speaking of sexual relations, let's talk about pedophiles for a minute. A pedophile is a person who loves children, and most teachers love children. I believe there needs to be a line that teachers will not cross in their love for children. Schools need to crack down on sexual attractions and lusting after middle school students. Also, high school students are prey also. If a teacher has fallen in love, then that teacher needs to alert a counselor and the principal and get transferred to another school or another classroom. No teenager, girl or boy, should need to deal with adult pedophile predators. People who chase after love or their romantic fantasies ought to be seen as predators, because that is what they are. Their pushiness probably scares a teen into consenting or playing along with this person out of pity or fear.

Predators are mentally unstable and a victim should never be blamed. Too many 13 year olds are getting romantically involved with their attractive teachers. There are good pedophiles who will not go there with a child, and there are bad pedophiles who want a child like a hungry wolf wants lamb chops. In some cases the feelings are real. Teachers need to get stronger and more focused about their role in a teenager's life and future. Sex should never enter the classroom. Sex always destroys, I repeat—sex always destroys discipline and concentration, in a co-ed setting. A teenager who will be looking towards freedom will not be looking at adults for sex partners. There are pre-teens already having sex with each other. America, take the blinders off. We already have small children molesting each other during slumber parties.

Some call the game "Doctor." Sex is a part of being human. There is no way to stop sex from happening, but at least be aware, stop acting like it does not exist. Puberty is pretty strong at 12 years old and some of our children are beginning puberty as young as 8. Some people blame the hormones in meat and dairy products. There is no controlling puberty, or a natural-born sex drive. Children are human beings, they are not robots and they deserve respect. Education has become an excuse to demand that children stop acting human and follow a life plan. Parents seethe with loathing and rage when a girl becomes pregnant. No one is getting married to raise men and women who will serve God in this century. Dr. Phil, a TV-show host, has had clients who locked their daughters in the bedroom so they could not go out of the house. With the internet, 13 year olds are finding anyone to love, desperate and starved for affection, they run away from home with a perfect stranger. Love and reproduction are basic human instincts that parents had better get ready to handle.

Teen aged children need responsibility, not just chores in the house, they also need a way to contribute to the family income in order to feel happy and whole. There is no joy or security when one person is working two jobs just to make ends meet and this able-bodied 13 year old young adult just sits in the bedroom watching TV, gossiping on social media and sleeping all day on Saturday. With zero furniture/telephones in the home, an unmarried mother will work two jobs and sleep all day to recuperate. The neighborhood will likely be scarey with a helping of violence served every weekend. All to help her children do better than she did, if she manages to maintain a clean and sober lifestyle. Poor children must go to school and become something better than a custodian or a nurse's aide. Why?

The standard might be a little too high. "Jack" and "Taco" are not jobs to sneer your nose at. A job in your hands is better than a job in your dreams. Jobs are all about survival, no matter how small or entry level. While sober single parents work hard with great sacrifices to make ends meet, their teens struggle with the guilt and shame of sitting on their gluten all day and night, dreaming of the future while raking in zero financial support. Sex? Really? Poor girls have seen or heard of women who were killed or enslaved by a boyfriend or husband. Poor girls who have a strong sense of survival are not likely to want to have casual relationships just because they are living on their own. They will want to keep their lives as simple and uncomplicated as possible.

We are letting the government and child psychologists tell us how to raise our children. They do not have a clue what the children are going through in their minds and what the parents are going through. Laws are supposed to serve and protect society, not the other way around. Tell America's Department of Child Labor and the United Nations thanks, but no thanks.

Give a 13er an opportunity to work a part-time job, and an opportunity to be influenced and guided into living a sober and moral lifestyle. Some laws need to be challenged in order for oppressed people groups to survive. People who have crossed a border for a better future know what I mean. There is a war of wills going on, a serious power struggle. These are the main years that parents can bring a legacy to their children and get respect for their experiences in life. If someone is declared an adult by law and knows they are not ready for disciplined responsibility and living on their own, then they are more than likely to listen to and honor their parent's guidance.

A lot of those juvenile delinquents who secretly smoked, drank, cursed and had sex at the age of 13 went on to become hard working adults. We label young people who rebel against their parents domination with an umbrella brush stroke, "JUVENILE DELINQUENTS." Then we wonder why the so-called GOOD KIDS are not thriving. They cannot seem to keep a good paying job, or stay in a good relationship, or parent one child without mother's help after the age of 21. Always losing a job and returning home to mother, or losing a caretaker boyfriend and returning to "Aunt Madea's" house. Human beings do not survive well with too much love and pampering. Human beings need a little bit of difficulty in their formative years. I am not saying "neglect and abandonment" are good for us, but there is such a thing as "too much coddling and protecting." We need 13 year olds to have choices to pack up and move out on their own, go out and look for a job and keep that job. There are many laws in place, 911 emergency dispatch, strong police departments, viable court systems and equal opportunity workplace laws that did not exist back in 1900.

An academy award winning actress named Jennifer Lawrence exemplifies what I am talking about, I hope she writes an autobiography someday. On a TV interview with 60 minutes, Sunday, August 5, 2018, I was absolutely fascinated that at the age of 14, about 10 years ago, she could no longer hold back on her God given gift and calling in life. Instead of enrolling in a high school, she went from Kentucky to New York and got acting jobs. She broke records with her Hunger Games sequels and other leading lady roles. She is getting paid doing what she loves most in life. She is not unhappily married or encumbered with a flock of fatherless children. When her parents trusted her to control her life, she did not seek a husband, she sought a career. Now she is living a dream.

CHAPTER TWO

LEGALIZING 13

"When I was a child, I spoke as a child, I understood as a child, I thought as a child, but when I became a man, I put away childish things." 1 Corinthians 13:11

Someone born with "silver spoons" in the kitchen might not have all the information necessary to create policy about child labor and age of majority for all citizens. For America's underprivileged and poor people, it is common sense survival to raise up children who will do housework, run to the store with money in hand and who will carry on some adult responsibilities towards raising a family and keeping a neat and organized household.

In 1900, a book written by Upton Sinclair opened the world's eyes to the exploitation of children working in meat factories. From that book child labor laws were developed and made it illegal to hire young people under 16 for full time work. In 1900 most of those working children were the bread winners in their families. Because of Upton Sinclair's book that exposed child abuse in meat factories that sometimes resulted in deaths, child labor laws were created.

Another reason for age limit law might be linked to a movie titled "Peyton Place" where a teen girl had an illegal medical abortion of a rape/incest baby. She was a pitiful young lady, traumatized and innocent of any wrongdoing. Forcing all teens to remain "jail bait" until age 18 and putting their sexual desires in a straight jacket could be the blanket vindication for what this fictional Peyton Place teen girl suffered. It is unfortunate that all children were thrown together in a group with the flourish of a pen with no distinction between old enough and too young. Setting in motion the mess that we have today. Of course I would not want 11 year-olds and under trying to be adults unless that child is intellectually and physically gifted. It is a matter of survival that a 13 year old become capable of being left home alone for several days at a time without getting into any kind of trouble in the neighborhood.

Poor parents need their adolescent children to help with the income within the limits of the law and their physical capabilities. Such as summer jobs and part time work at a restaurant or car wash. The most negative thing of all is babyish 13ers and apathetic parents. We need to move on with our lives and stop catering to the late bloomers and parents who just don't care. This present policy does just that. I believe 13 years of "mental slavery" and "mindless submission" to unrelated adults (and their abuses of their authority) is long enough. The Oscar Award winning movie titled <u>FENCES</u>, illustrates what I am talking about. It is not in any way healthy fighting with a person who does not want your parenting. Denzel Washington's character clearly demonstrates the futility of yelling and screaming in order to be heard by an 18 year-old son who already closed his mind to further parenting from his father.

In a worse case scenario; a loving mom is nude dancing and turning tricks, not for pleasure but to pay the rent, while her three lazy, disrespectful teen sons are sitting up in their bedrooms not even asking about her, but caring only about themselves. They are done with physical growth, the youngest is 13; 5'5" tall weighing 150 pounds, but because of mandatory school attendance and age limit laws, all three young men are sitting up watching TV and eating chips, after less than 30 minutes of homework. They will not do anything their mother asks them kindly to do. She is a prisoner in her own home, working to care for these three self-centered, ungrateful and intimidating half-grown men she gave birth to with love in her heart. Now she is counting the hours, days and months until the last one turns 18. This loving little mother, pretty and petite, is out after dark supplementing the income of a minimum wage job, on a six hour night shift at a sleazy topless bar, with three teen boys sitting at home, not even the common decency to clean the apartment. That is a sin in front of God. How dare these politicos yell "entitlement mentality". The age limit laws set this up.

What if this is a government conspiracy against America's poor and uneducated? Like legalized abortion. Like the birth control pill. Like sex education classes. Nevertheless, there will always be determined young people choosing to remain in school and attend a university at all costs, hoping to overcome poverty. Chasing after a dream job because poverty is like a deadly disease. When a child who is poor is left home alone from the age of 6-years old, mornings and evenings, that child has a different mind from a middle-class or rich kid counterpart. Without age 13 emancipation, their hands are tied towards helping their guardians or parents deal with their poverty.

When caught working legitimate jobs to stay away from crime, 13-year olds get labeled "Juvenile Delinquents" and all they are trying to do is survive. The rights I am proposing for 13 year olds are not to disrupt happy homes, or functional homes, but TO BETTER THE WORST OF LIVING CONDITIONS for most inner city teenagers. They do not have a fighting chance with straight jacket laws that control them from working and taking on self responsibility.

What about reversals of fortune? What does she do when she is let go from a job? Or what if she goes out with friends and tries a hit of crack just to fit in, but becomes addicted? How many friends and relatives can she count on to house her thirteen year-old while she runs the streets searching for a way to earn money for drugs? In <u>"USA TODAY-LIFELINE BIOGRAPHIES: TUPAC SHAKUR. HIP-HOP IDOL"</u>, it tells a story about a gifted young teen who had an unstable childhood. He was birthed and raised by a single parent who had difficulty with illegal narcotics and holding down a job and keeping a roof over their heads. She would take him from house to house to live with relatives and close friends while he attended school. He would make friends with teens who stayed out of trouble. He would do well in his classes and then get uprooted without any preparation.

He gave his fans an image of hatred towards Caucasians in his music and the children he was the closest to were Caucasians. He was really a Black geek, or worse he would have been rejected by the many Black fans he had. They would have called him a "sell-out". The lack of emotional security had a negative impact on the young man. The young man was Tupac Shakur. *Tupac went to Rolling Park Junior High until eighth grade. Then he earned a spot at the famous Baltimore School for the Arts… Tupac was sad that he had to quit BSA. Leaving that school affected me so much he said. Even now, I see that as the point where I got off track.*" I boldly declare if Tupac Shakur could have lived on his own at 13, he might be alive today.

The absence of human and civil rights for 13ers helps to maintain a status quo of unhappy endings. Our America is being fruitful and multiplying young adults who experience imprisonment, sex trafficking, mental illness and homelessness. Hypothetically, as soon as they steal a loaf of bread or a pair of shoes from the store, they get a cold cement cage, 10' by 10', with cold iron bars on the door. The bed is a stainless steel half of a 50 pound drum welded into the concrete wall. There's a stainless steel toilet and sink at the foot of the bed with no curtain for privacy, all adding insults to the injuries.

The negatives of letting 13ers have adult rights have been so highly magnified since 1900 that the United States of America has been pushing for other countries to raise their legal age to 18 also. They act like the worse thing a 13 year-old can do is get married and raise a family, hold down a job and pay their own bills. Funny thing about an age, it only lasts 12 months. A myriad of opportunities for love and career slip away for some gifted young adults between ages 13 and 18.

Very few men want a fully mature and educated woman who can compete for leadship in running the household. If all a girl wants to do is get married and raise children, it is morally wrong to interfere with that dream. It is her dream, no one has a right to take that away from her. Perhaps, with help from her family and friends, she can have it all. She can continue her education and work a job, while being there for her children and her husband. I believe in the "Right to Try." Since we Americans refuse to rear our children to become independent at the age of 13, the negatives of being 13 and independent continue to pop up in the daily news.

The 13ers would try to take up the slack with their natural faith in God and themselves to just do what their hearts tell them, if only they had the cultural permission to do SO.

Thirteen year olds getting married before making a baby is nothing new in many UN countries, but it is a thought of blasphemy in 21st Century America where education has replaced God's will for our children's lives. Most Muslim and Latino nations are not following in the United States' footsteps. Why would they want to set themselves up for endangerment or genocide? Why would they want to become a matriarchy? Why would they want a society in which a married man never gets a virgin bride?—but she is wearing white anyway, unaware or uncaring of the meaning. Why would they follow advice that guarantees divorces and single parenting for a lifetime?

It's a miracle how teens keep putting up with child abuse until the age of 18, then leave home without expressing hatred for their guardians. What is the real reason for pushing adulthood forward another 5 years? What parent in their right mind agrees to keep their 13 year old daughter at home not contributing to the home another 5 years, instead of finding her a good young man to court, marry and get out of the house with? Who are the full grown adults who enjoy the arguments, fussing and fighting with 13 year old sons who want to go out and do as they please because they feel like they are men? What kind of a law makes a man tell his 13 year old, 6 foot, 200 pound sons, they are too young to get a job full time and put school at part-time no matter how destitute they might be?

Emancipation is a step in the right direction. Should America consider emancipating 13 year old Juvenile Delinquents? Most of them have some kind of complaint against their parents. Should they be allowed to parent themselves? Eventually they will be legal to live on their own, can they self-govern once they become legal adults? Will they look to their parents for the rest of their lives to get them out of their messes? Will they get addicted to welfare and unemployment? What is wrong with locking them in their rooms and forcing them to go on the Dr. Phil Show? Dr. Phil has a very good track record for turning rebel teens around. Some of what the U.S.A. is calling "Juvenile Delinquents" is actually young people trying to survive in a social structure that refuses to see them as done with being children. I believe something leaves the soul when a young person "cooperates" in his or her own "soul reduction," something of God gets lost in that process. Could this be a version of The Stockholm Syndrome?

Even children need space, some parents control and punish too much. They want their children to be angels 100% of the time. They punish their children for being a certain way in personality as opposed to simply "doing something that is morally wrong." They use corporal punishment as a means of "fixing and molding" their children. Nola Peacock writes extensively about doing too much for children, on being "Helicopter Parents." In her book, "<u>HONOURING OUR KIDS</u>..." Nola Peacock makes this comment: *"As parents, we may imagine that we want perfectly obedient children who will do everything we tell them to and just follow along. But that's the last thing you want, because then they're going to blindly follow along with their peers, and that's not a good thing. If kids are constantly expected to DO AS THEY'RE TOLD, they will. This may include doing what their peers or adults in authority (like coaches and teachers) tell them. This can set them up to be abused or treated poorly."*

We have a generation of divorced and unwed mothers of poverty and welfare benefits that have co-parented about three generations of children with teachers at school. There is an answer, and there is a hope. Even though there are age limits, encourage your sons and your daughters to get summer jobs and do whatever it takes to keep those jobs through the school year. Success comes from holding on to a job, do not eat the lies of this crazy government, college debt will devour your leftover income from your minimum wage job. Very few companies are hiring minorities and people born and raised in poverty who have a college diploma. You know what they ask you, guess, here it comes, "Do you have experience?"

College is not your hope, Jack-n-the-Box and other jobs like it will be your hope. Let your child start from the entry level job and keep on working until they will have no other choice but make your son or daughter the owner or manager. Let your 13er hold on to a job, no matter how small it may seem. America owes a debt of gratitude to the rebels and juvenile delinquents who never got caught drinking, smoking, cursing and laying with teachers. They put on a pretense to keep their parents happy and behind closed doors they stopped being pure and innocent. By the time 18 came around they were more than ready to leave home and make sound decisions for their lives. Most juvenile delinquents are caught up in a lifestyle against their better judgment and the way they were raised. Job opportunities for 13 year olds would help alleviate and bring down the numbers of 13 year old delinquents.

Not every child will respond to emancipation, many of them will stay babyish and co-dependent on parents. Good parents should not abuse that loyalty. All the teens really need is a choice to quit school for a little while and work a full time job to help their mother get a car and buy new clothes, just for starters. Taxpayer dollars go to support Juvenile Detention facilities. So many of those criminals are not criminals at all. Just abused teens who do not have anywhere to turn. In a better culture, the abuser would be incarcerated and the teens would be allowed to govern themselves, with some professional supervision such as case-workers making sure they are doing well. There are 13 year-olds leaving home because of abuse and running with real thieves and murderers.

Prostitution is not women's liberation. Servicing the perversions and sexual fantasies of random strangers, males, females, homosexuals, lesbians and freaks, is not a sane career choice, so do not get me twisted. It is pathetic how many of our sons and daughters are being put on the sidewalk looking sweet and innocent for the new prostitution system and police are paid off to look the other way, the money is more than the national treasury. Morality might not pay as well as crime, but you can hold your head up, be proud of your job and have peace with God. Immorality is the handmaid of this legal age policy. Why do they teach sex education instead of marriage navigation and child development? Why do they have no problem showing our children how to put a condom on a banana? Wouldn't this be against the law outside of the classroom? Why do schools get immunity from prosecution for corrupting minors?

Homes that are not stable enough to assist young people who wish to attend school, should be dismantled without going back and forth.

Problem adults with drug and alcohol addictions can take a lifetime getting straightened out. Incest should be judged by the aggravating factors, number of years and trauma to the child. Those adults should never again be allowed to have custody of their children. All children need a "right now" safe environment, not long term promises. This is what I am talking about, parents who cannot take care of their children and the children who will resort to crime to survive. Americans can do better than this.

Most young people who shoot and kill people see themselves as adults in small bodies. That smallness in size is usually temporary, but the murder or armed robbery is permanent. Rebellious 13ers might not continue in their delinquent ways. The right to adulthood might encourage them to behave better. They will not have the "too young to go to prison" excuse motivating them. They might very well discontinue doing crimes. Treating them like a little kid who deserves leniency is what they count on. Removing that glitch in the criminal justice system might bring down the crime rate among teenagers. We already have detention centers for teens in place. They will simply have longer sentences so justice will be served, not curbed because of someone's age, they knew right from wrong and chose to do the wrong, there needs to be consequences.

Hypothetically, if a 13 year old fails to thrive in college, or in the workforce, or in a marriage with babies to raise, then parents should be welcome to intervene or any adults close to the situation. Teens run away from their parents at this legal age of 18 to avoid the scrutiny and domination that they endured for five years. Unless they have parents like the Duggar family. Many move out on their 18" birthday and put their parents out of their minds. They do not call or write. They create a fake family background, all because of the domination that they went through when they felt like they wanted to take control of their lives at age 13 but feared the consequences. Also, it would help if these teens could run away from criminal parents without being returned to them or being thrown into juvenile detention. Identifying them before the age of 13 and ascertaining if they are being influenced by their criminal home environment would help deter the creation of a criminal adult.

A child should have a right to a crime-free home, neighborhood, or environment. These rights would help this segment of society in a tremendous way by allowing them alternatives to the negativity of intolerable domestic situations. A 13 year old juvenile delinquent doesn't care what the law says and will do as she or he pleases. Good young people are suffering the most from these age limit laws. If the adulthood age is 13, then there is hope to restore a family if parents have changed from their criminal ways. We are a society of too much government. Government is controlling our lives for so many different reasons. Population can be controlled by starting a war and drafting all the unmarried teen aged boys. These boys are seen as expendable by the government. Of course the government wants to keep 13ers single. If they get killed or maimed it is okay because nobody loved them and they were not fathers to anyone. Also, they did not have jobs, so they did not lead productive lives in the first place. At least fighting in a war kept them from becoming criminals. Keep the draft age at 18 while 13ers get married, buy homes and help their wives raise babies.

Where we are now, entire families are committing genocide with secret teen abortions and a "misogamy subculture." (Misogamy means hatred for marriage.) The smarter they are the more they want to be free. So they are forced to stay home with their parents until they turn 18. A home that feels like a prison brings anger. Parents saying and emphasizing that the teen owes them everything and owns nothing breeds a sense of hopelessness and failure even before the teen gets started at becoming an independent adult. Hurt feelings tend to grow seeds of anger and frustration. The fruit of anger brings dishonor, deceit, disloyalty and sometimes hate in its many forms. I believe one of the reasons that some teenagers are angry is the stress forced upon them to keep attending school. Then they continue their anger in their adult years. They sometimes decide to end it all and take a few people with them, breaking news. We can save some lives by emancipating 13 year olds.

In this advanced age of technology and genius as normal, not one single parent has publicly demanded a shortened period for childhood. After 18 years of sitting idle and not doing anything productive, young people are expected to tackle living away from their parents and making their own decisions, including who to marry. Parents have warehoused their own children. Parents have not spent enough quality time with their sons and daughters that would counter-attack the damage of 18 years of "junk food" education, self-centeredness and not working at a full time job. Quite a few teens have compared their fathers to wardens and their homes to prisons. Giving 13 year olds adult rights is not all about sex, because some teens have homosexual or developmental disabilities and are not at all interested in sexual relationships. Mainly it is the safety net of being free from mom and dad telling them what to do all the time. It is simply a legal right TO LEAVE THE NEST.

Freedom means a lot to all adults. Children do not normally want or desire the absence of mom and dad, but young adults do. The smarter they are, the more they want to be free. Why not choose happiness for everyone? Let that 13er go. Put them in their own apartment and wait for them to seek advice, don't nose into their business. Let them be responsible for all their bad decisions. Even if it means jail or prison. See why religion is important? They need an all knowing, ever present father figure who is forgiving, nonjudgmental, moved by worship and works miracles. Prolonging childhood another five years has been forced on the majority of America's young people far too long, like some kind of an experiment. Of course there are negatives to giving adulthood to people barely old enough to handle stress and pressure. Some are still growing and maturing, that is a negative, but that could be seen of many 18 year olds. The point here is that a 13er can be reigned in with love and kindness, not yet hardened by 5 years of neglect and abandonment.

Our culture has trained poor American children and immigrants to care only about themselves and making money in the future. They ignore their parents and their present problem of poverty. No one cares to honor their parents in their pursuit of the American Dream. What is wrong with loyalty to your family and helping your parents? As long as it isn't a crime, what is wrong with parents training their children to work a family business at the age of 13? We are hurting our country with these laws that tell an individual you cannot work a full time job and sign a lease and live by yourself at age 13. What is wrong with leaving high school to work a legitimate full time job to help your parents, or your single parent pay the bills? Not a God Blessed thing! This is why delinquency will rise at an all time high by next century. These young people are learning quickly and maturing faster than past generations.

They will refuse to be held back by laws that do not make any sense. Laws are supposed to help people, not hurt them. This is a law that only helps criminals avoid the consequences of their crimes by calling them juveniles. It also stops girls from getting married and or making rational decisions about their sex drive. It encourages prostitution and a promiscuous lifestyle. It also supports abortions, condoms, contraceptive foams, sponges, birth control pills and the STD drug industry. There is very little moral value being supported by prolonging childhood. You cannot get married, give birth to your own children and raise up those children in your own home, paid for by your own hard earned money from a good moral job. When 13 year olds have a baby it goes to adoption in most households. Naturally, a 13 year old is a child also. A baby raising a baby. It is not the end of the world for these young teens. They will need financial support and common sense guidance, but it will be for all the right reasons. If there is sex with an adult, the adult goes to jail, even if it was mutual consent or love.

There are adults who can graduate from college because of a photographic memory, but they are stunted in their maturity and capable of falling in love with a 13er. Do we have a right to judge that? If the kid is happy, shouldn't we just make sure that the adult does not abuse the kid? Why should we make an uproar like we were jealous of such a pairing? We have too many rules, rules that are morally destructive and that contribute to criminal behavior and juvenile delinquency. Catch this adult in the act and give him or her an ultimatum, "do not use my child for a sex toy, marry this child and be good to him or her, pay for emotional damages and therapy, or go straight to jail" If the child was not physically harmed, give the adult the sentence of a prostitute, six months. Be fair about it and don't brand this seduced adult a sex offender. If this was a love affair with only one child, a first time thing, initiated by the child who saw him or herself as an adult, then it should not be dealt with harshness.

I hope and pray that the USA will one day evolve enough to understand that there are children who are pretending to be pure and innocent. Thirteen year olds who cannot get a job do not have any choice but to go whole heartedly into organized crime. The current system refuses to allow employers to work them full time at an entry level job position. So a genius IQ gets wasted in criminal enterprises. Our tax dollars pay for juvenile detention centers. It is not a prison, but it is what prison ought to be. An apartment with kind looking guards, more like foster care, but the bedrooms have iron doors with bars. Even the kids who murder people go to the same holding facility as the kid who ran away from home. Crime is not always in the heart and soul of a human being. Humane surroundings should be the goal of prison reform, not the exception, and not just reserved for the rich and privileged. When taking on an adult role with its responsibilities would make their life better and solve some problems, age limit laws create problems in their lives.

Kids who are trying to take care of themselves get a criminal record and a juvenile delinquent label for a lifetime just for taking on adulthood against the law. They are not bad people, but they are smart kids following their hearts. They spend their day in a classroom setting in juvenile detention, learning things as though they were in high school. It is better than the home that could not control them, but they are not free to leave. There is also the danger of getting raped and molested, just like in adult prison. It is to scare them straight. Why are we locking kids up who run from their parents? Why aren't the parents being checked for child abuse or neglect or plain old lack of competence? When will this country stop treating teens like a parent's property?

When taking on an adult role with its responsibilities would make life better, the age limit laws block rescue. America has the power to make up its mind to help children survive their households of poverty, crime and abandonment. Being labeled a juvenile delinquent might be a small price to pay for leaving a home of rapes and beatings. What about the thousands of young boys and girls who commit suicide or become sex workers or predators? We are a country where some lesbians and transgender women have fought for all women to have "equality" in paychecks and opportunities, being misinterpreted as an attack against all heterosexual men raised to take care of a wife and children.

Somewhere in the U.S.A. there was a "gang-rape" of a 13 year old girl and it was put in the news. She was raped on her school campus, alone at night, in a prom dress. She never had any idea that boys and men looked at her in that kind of way. She could have been more careful, carried her prom clothes and heels in a tote bag while wearing blue jeans, flats and a large sweat-shirt with a hoodie jacket. Why hasn't co-ed education produced young men who respect women? Why all this raping? This experiment of mixing teen boys and girls in the same classrooms is a failure and when will we just stop it? No voices of authority have even bothered to consider that sexcentric schooling contributes to misogyny, sexual harassment and date rape. Familiarity breeds contempt, in general, disrespect for all women. Here is a possible reason why there are men from good homes and backgrounds who do not respect women. Think about it.

Teaching little boys in classes around America to pull out chairs and open doors for girls and ladies. MIGHT BE part of the reason women are dehumanized and despised by men when they are fully matured adults. "Gender difference" training MIGHT BE keeping men in disrespect of women. Women have been "roaring" since the 1970's so why so much rape and so much sexual harassment? There are single moms who adore their sons up until they buck against why he should "cater to" a lady friend of hers. Why should someone's little boy be pulling up chairs, carrying things and opening doors for females they cannot marry? The common denominator that has not changed with men and boys is this incessant "gender difference" training. Why still make a distinction about who opens a door, pulls up a chair or helps a lady with her groceries? See, these things can be shared by both genders. Whoever is the tallest, the strongest or the healthiest bears the burden of helping. Should not put it out there like manhood, or men only.

Are we teaching 8 year old boys to open the doors and pull out the chairs for just the pretty 8 year old girls, to get their attention? Adults are so impressed and charmed, they think this is so cute. It just means so much to adults, but it means "Phooey" to little girls. Little girls who sneer at the sight of little boys and call them "dumb and ugly." I do not agree with it. Why put little boys in a position to be laughed at and ridiculed by little girls. You can be sure that they are getting picked on, mocked, ridiculed when adults are not around. It is thoughtless and mindless to teach these "men only" behaviors too soon.

The best age to teach chivalry is 11, a border age near puberty. Around 11 a lot of boys are just beginning to notice girls. That will give the young men an advantage and help them be attractive to a lonely preteen girl. No little boy should be holding the door for every woman who walks into a building, that is just wrong, stop teaching that. When those boys reflect upon being mistreated by little girls, surely they get angry. I would not encourage a boy under 13 (or who hates girls) to pull chairs and open doors for any and all girls and women because he is only a child and he is very likely to retaliate against mean girls who do not smile and say "Thank you." It MIGHT BE contributing to the hatred, sexualization and disrespect some men have for all women and girls. Perhaps in their eyes, women are too powerful and too important and give nothing back. Women just take and take. Mothers initiate divorce, mothers leave the home, mothers stress fathers for child support. Mothers control everything and fathers get nothing back in return for being good providers. It MIGHT BE causing some of our boys to adopt an attitude of loathing towards all females.

Teaching a small boy before puberty that his manhood depends on helping women sit in chairs and open doors, MIGHT BE the catalyst for a lifetime of woman hating. For a more positive response, teach the small boy that door holding is for anyone who might be weaker than ourselves, or smaller than ourselves, as an act of Christian favor and compassion. It makes more sense to teach boys to open doors and pull chairs as part of the courtship relationship towards a girl they plan to marry one day and Christian helpfulness, but not to extremes. They might respond better if door opening is seen as a part of being a Christian, not as a mandatory manhood behavior. They must be allowed to discriminate who they will open a door for or pull out a chair for or carry groceries and books for.

Keep in mind that there are boys who should not be encouraged to hold the door like a doorman for ten or more perfect strangers who happen to be women and girls. This is not appropriate in my point of view. What is the message here? How can boys grow to like girls when they are being taught to serve girls by opening doors and pulling out chairs for them? Where is the payback, the reward? There is none. How can boys be expected to like girls when manhood is being measured by the ability or willingness to open doors and pull out chairs for every female in the room? No one gives them a reward. Too soon before they reach 13 they are being forced to act all chivalrous and no one will give them a hug, smile or kiss. Perfect strangers should not expect your husband or boyfriend to hold a door for them. Chivalry should be seen as a desirable character trait, not a con game. Boys should choose to adopt chivalry, not have it forced on them through sternness or coercion.

There are men who cannot believe in women to lead armies, run government agencies or pilot airplanes because of a hurtful childhood experience that may have originated from such an aggressive act as pulling out a chair or holding a door open. We must work harder to prepare our children for the workplace. Mindless chivalry is hurting us. Women are still being molested, groped and raped on college campuses and at work. Something has got to give. We are a "rape is sex" nation constantly putting rape victims on Social Security for depression, personality disorders and PTSD. More and more grown up and educated women have no choice but to apply for Social Security because "being a rape victim" has destroyed their trust in men and their ability to socialize freely in the workplace with men who are perfect strangers. We keep training our sons to see all women as physically weak and they work harder when women are around picking up the slack for women employees. Weak women need to lift weights and eat protein like weak men do. That is the price of equality.

We lack programs in our culture that help women learn self-defense and be aware of putting themselves in situations, alone with a male co-worker, relative, classmate, teacher, minister, priest, cab/bus driver, etc... I once requested to have a chaperone in the exam room because being alone with a strange man brings bad memories and the doctor rescheduled me with a female. Raping and molesting women might be felt as a way of taking back all that power that women had over their lives growing up, over their masculine identity and their confidence in manhood. Sympathy is already leading to decriminalization of rape and incest. Forcing these antiquated gendercentric customs on our little boys is not in their best interest. We might be inadvertently raising women haters.

The worse prohibition of all is that 13ers cannot run away from an abusive home. An abused child goes into survival mode when being raped, beaten or molested at home. Without the support that legalizing age 13 brings, these young people stay in the worse of lifestyles waiting to turn 18. With the baggage of an entire childhood of being abused by an evil adult they might become career criminals and atheists. They might create a new identity and cut off all ties and connections to their bloodlines, or they might commit suicide or serial murder. It would take a strong will to be a good person and not do any one of those things.

Pedophile adults should not be the reason to withhold adulthood or emancipation from 13 year olds. We have too many ways to communicate, educate and create awareness to protect young people. Background checks on behavior towards the opposite sex should influence whether a boy is unfit to be in a co-ed classroom and have easy access to females. There is a dark side to American families no one wants to talk or think about. The worst thing we could do is decriminalize rape and incest and tell a survivor to get over it just because rape victims like Oprah Winfrey and Joyce Meyer are rich and famous and don't seem to be mentally suffering. We need a "Caught Red Handed" law that allows Good Samaritans or family members to do a citizen's arrest of a pedophile sex abuser caught in the act. A runaway who complains about incest should be taken seriously, not ignored. Detectives should put cameras in the room or put a wire on the child. A pro-active approach will send a message in the culture that incest and rape are inexcusable and will be prosecuted to the fullest extent of the law.

TV evangelist, Joyce Meyer, is a living witness to incest from age "too young to remember" to age 18. The kind of incest that most men get killed for when caught doing it. I strongly believe if Joyce Meyer could have been emancipated at age 13 she would have moved out and got away from this abuse, instead she endured the terrorism until she turned 18, the age she could legally move out.

This is why I am writing this book, because I strongly believe choices will protect children. When the law says "You are not old enough at 13", that kills choices.

CHAPTER THREE

IDEAS FOR BETTER EDUCATION

"Turn away my eyes from looking at worthless things and revive me in Your way."

Psalm 119:3 7

Education will always be needed in our society. Without it we run the risk of going backwards and losing the great progress that makes our country a potentially decent place for all human beings to live. We have too much to lose. However, I have a problem with underestimating the value of a good education. I also have a problem with forced learning and putting children in unsafe and uncomfortable classrooms. Bullying, will always be a problem. The very first thing a small sweet child encounters is a big mean child. The learning environment needs to be safe. Teachers lusting after attractive students is also a problem. Maybe the single teacher classroom needs to be re-evaluated. There needs to be a check and a balance. When I was in Karate School someone would check on the classroom every 15 to 20 minutes. The teacher knew he could not get away with unprofessional behavior. I took that for granted, now I am very glad for it. Teachers lusting after students and having off-hour time with the students, unsupervised, should not be tolerated or covered up. There needs to be a check and balance, hidden cameras or classroom tapes, hallway recordings or an undercover snitch. Sex education was a bad idea 50 years ago and it is now a very bad idea.

Most importantly, parents depend on a public school facility to be their free babysitting service. Especially working mothers and single parents. It has been hurting us for some time that children are getting out of school around 2PM while their guardians are still working, often overtime, on their jobs. Now cooperative children will stay inside and keep all the doors locked, living in fear of strangers until an adult gets home. The rebellious children will refuse to care and just go running around all over the neighborhood looking for something to do. Schools have been ignoring this for years. The very reason I think it is time to consider 13 an age of adulthood and get this group of young people interested in working jobs, if only they had a right to work. Another thing that would help society and 13 year olds, if schools stayed open until 6PM and provided a small meal for those students who go home to emptiness and lack of supervision. They could work on their school work, play sports in the gym, or socialize with friends. Also, there should be a 2 to 40 ratio of teacher supervision ideally.

[KINDERGARTEN, AGES 2-5] We have so many people coming in from undeveloped countries, that it is very likely children will begin their lives in homes where both parents are working just to keep up with the basics of a comfortable lifestyle. A family with children of different ages will best be served by schools that include babies in one of their buildings. Also, last but not least, high-schools for this millennium should have at least one daycare building and toddler playground for obvious reasons.

The first year of Kindergarten should be renamed "first grade". All levels of tax paid schooling should be seen as legitimate and viable. Kindergarten (or Head Start) gives the impression that all they do is play, eat cookies and take naps. It is nearly a miracle to get them to obey commands, to calm down and let some stranger tell them what to do. It is innately the most difficult, not the easiest level of educating children. Kindergartners should wear a unisex uniform. Gender differences are very distracting, especially dresses versus pants. Put the girls in a feminine version of what the boys wear. Allow the girls to be themselves, not burdened with what grown women are expected to be like around grown men. Under the age of 7 is much too young for patronizing the opposite gender. In other words, separate the boys from the girls so they can move freely and concentrate on learning.

[BASIC ELEMENTARY SCHOOL, AGES 6-9] Homosexuality is perfectly normal in children under the ages before puberty, and hating the opposite gender is perfectly normal at this stage of life. Interfering with natural transgender behavior in childhood development apparently creates abnormality in mental development and sets up personality disorders and depression problems. Transgender children who keep drawing attention to their disability might best be served in the Special Education department. Restrooms should be designed so that boys and girls do not accidentally walk into each other's restrooms.

[MIDDLE SCHOOL, AGES 10-12] I would prefer gay men teaching the girls and lesbians teaching the boys as they become a part of the public education system. It is getting more and more difficult to trust so-called "straight people" as school teachers, because they cannot seem to be faithful to their husbands and wives when they have a "beautiful" 13er in their classroom. More and more we see in the media that straight teachers are falling in love with their students who they met in the kindergarten years. Right around the age that I want to have legalized, but that does not make it okay. It does prove to me that no government should be messing around with God's natural laws of growth, development, love and attractions. Two teachers in the classroom might also help curtail romance in 8th grade with teacher. Once again, when the children reach proficiency in the basics of reading, writing and arithmetic, they should be in a non-competitive atmosphere. No grades, no attaboys, treat learning like it is no big deal. Make learning a routine skill.

Encourage social skills that help them get jobs and hold on to relationships. Another alternative for public schools is separate schools for girls and gays together, since most of America's teen boys are wild like animals, believing they were descended from apes. The words Ladies and Gentlemen have lost meaning in this century.

Schools should be teaching young people to use their words. Violence should never be seen as a "problem solving skill." I would like to see all girls have equal access to weight lifting; football, wrestling, boxing, karate and basketball in all public schools, no buts about it. Report cards are meaningless to poor children, they need food, money, clothes and transportation. Report on their behavior, attitude, social skills, manners, etiquette, posture, giving encouraging words, helpfulness and such like.

School should be seen as an interruption of the real world, a mere distraction that does not control their lives. School should not be a place of being ridiculed, or labeled dumb or inferior. School should not become God. Children should not be getting stressed out about school. Education should not be a source of frustration to the point of tears or depression, it simply is not worth it. People think bullying isn't serious, but bullying can effect a child his or her entire life. On the flip side, children who get bullied might retaliate. We have seen the school shootings in the news.

Reward children with supplies, books, equipment, passes, tickets and gift cards, not the destructive fruits of competition. An artist forced to study history should be getting paid for it. The present system takes advantage of and pretty much abuses our children. It can't understand why we complain so much, why aren't poor people grateful for a school?

An Eighth Grade Diploma needs to be equal to a High School diploma, so that impatient young adults won't feel coerced into continuing to attend school, when they deeply desire to stay close to home. Kids that are burned out on school should feel free to decide to take a break after 8th Grade. Relax those child-labor laws for young people 14 years old. Allow ages 13 and 14 to be for job experience. Let these be years of transition from childhood of being taken care of, to adolescence in which they can do something towards taking care of themselves. They can take that lemonade stand a little more seriously, the baby-sitting jobs, the piano teaching, the fruit selling, the grass cutting and carport sweeping. Money is survival. Children who have gifts for working need not be held back. Also, this is a good time to be learning the rules of driving and to use video games that simulate driving skills. Some people who wait until age 15 cannot learn how to drive, because the "education burn-out" takes hold.

[HIGH SCHOOL, AGES 15-17] The atmosphere of most public high schools is so frightening and intimidating that given a choice a lot of teens would skip high school altogether and go straight to community college. High school is mostly good for the career goals of athletes, cheerleaders, scientists, dancers, singers, actors and musicians. The ordinary children get left out, they sit in the bleachers and applaud, or they duck and dodge the big campus bully. Without high school your 13er will be just fine from doing time until age 18. Legal age does not mean parents are no longer necessary. There are still social skills that good parents can always impart to their children. Whatever age we are, we are always our parents babies. Public high school has been destroying our country from within for at least 50 years. If we move quickly we can turn this country around and find our "God center" again. I suggest holding young people back a couple of years so they will be more independent of the peer pressure. Possibly more physically developed also.

High school is set up perfectly for premarital sex. Co-ed education is a terrible American custom. If you think for a minute your child will not be exposed to some kind of sexual assault or seductive language to participate in an orgy, threesome, or sex for barter, you are a perfectly dumb parent. Obviously it is pushed and supported by homophobics. The presence of females does not stop gay rapes, or molestation, girls and gays are equal in the mind of a predator.

The worse clothes a person can wear, male or female, are dresses and tunics without outerwear shorts or pants underneath. There is no protection in a flimsy piece of cloth wrapped like a napkin around your private parts. Your knees, thighs, calves and ankles are exposed to the elements and put on display. Girls should be encouraged to wear denim, corduroy or wool blend ankle length pants to school; leggings or skinny jeans (underneath those dresses or tunics) during the cool months. Like the boys, girls could wear Bermuda shorts during the hot months with a loose fitting cotton tee shirt. When will equality include clothing? We are the only country on Earth that requires sexiness of our daughters during their formative years, when will equality come? We have created a culture of sexual teasing in the clothes women wear. How will we ever be taken seriously? If sexual arousal, 24/7, is the only way women and men can get along, then this country is in real big trouble.

Let's just split it down the middle before we have blood in the streets. We have raised entire generations of female minds who think the answer to getting success is to dress like fashion models or look like porn stars. If women want equal pay, they need to stop being so sexy and manipulative towards every man and lesbian they meet. Straight men and lesbians will do a beauty queen's job for her, even in the Army. What is wrong with this picture? Also, high heels over 2 inches in public high school should be discouraged. In other words, teachers and students should not be wearing stilettos to class. Let us take "sexy" out of the learning environment. Just like a job wants us to focus and leave our escapes at home, the learning culture needs to discourage escapism and fantasy life on school campuses. Chris Palmer, "RAISE YOUR KIDS TO SUCCEED" says: *"Sexualization is an impediment to kids succeeding in school. When kids who are heavy consumers of popular culture are in school, they are likely to be thinking about sexually exploitative images instead of science or history or French. Girls especially are being encouraged by popular culture to present themselves as sex objects in order to please boys, when they should be focused on their studies and on learning…."*

American women are raised to see men as morally strong and their servants and protectors while wearing clothes that say "Come and get it". In high school, girls spend four years dreaming about marriage and babies, not becoming a lawyer, doctor or Walstreet broker. How is that preparation for adulthood? The boys spend four years posturing for a girl's attention while playing sports or being in the band or theater, how does that prepare them for adulthood? We don't need "promiscuous promenade" dances, we need adulthood and the mature behavior that comes with it. Parents are man-dated by the government to co-parent their next generation with school teachers. Their children are being shoved out of the house against their best judgment, like human encyclopedias, into Sodom and Gomorrah, aka high school, where ape-like behavior is tolerated. In her book, "<u>CHILDISM</u>", Elisabeth Young puts forth facts and statistics about this social trend towards a hatred of children. Quoting from her book: "*...So strong has been the anti-child trend, that every U.S. Congress since 1989, has refused to ratify the U.N. Convention on the Rights of the Child, the international community's pioneering effort to hold adults accountable for the well-being of their young...*" By the time these innocent ones finish high school (which is more like a prison than an institution of learning) they lose most of their moral virtue and behave worse than animals towards people they are attracted to and claim to love. Look at the stats on Domestic Violence, Divorce and Child Abuse, this is what "Love American Style" really means.

If 13 were the legal age, then the high schools could be converted into community colleges and mature behavior would be encouraged. Proper attire and treating people well would be expected to prepare for the work force. What we have right now is a party atmosphere: anything goes, flirty behavior is encouraged, bullying is the order of the day and who can wear the skimpiest clothes, weirdest tattoos and razed hair. No one is doing anything about it. No one is addressing it. Some businesses have actually had to lower their standards of professional attire and hair requirements because the young people are hard wired to act like they did in high school and dress like they did in high school.

[COLLEGE PREP, AGES 19-20] Let 18 be a year of earning money at a job, socializing and reconnecting with being human. Start college preparatory school at the of 19 and make it a two year curriculum with classes directly linked with the universities in the state for college credit. Split the tax money for high schools. States could turn those high schools into mini-colleges with supervised emergency dorm rooms for children growing up in homes of crime and abandonment. They all graduate high school Less of an adult and less moral than when they were 8th graders. They may have been abused, molested or sexualized because of their home environment, and they are expected to suck it up and go to school like nothing is wrong. All the while hating parental authority figures and their lives of learned hopelessness.

This segment of education should be for gifted children who will go on to college and be successful with a college degree. Now pull out all the stops and let the whole world know how smart you. This should be the students who want to be in school, who have a goal towards college and who strongly wish to get along with everybody for good references and networking. In "UNDERSTANDING YOUR GIFTED CHILD...", written by Dr. James Delisle: "*...They had come to see this young man as lazy, disheveled, and obstinate; yet the few times Jeff did shine were when he was allowed to do projects of personal interest or open-ended assignments with multiple right answers—or no right answers at all....*" Make no mistake about it, those five years between 13 and 18, are a lifetime for some of America's young people. A stretch of time that a few of our children will not survive. Like ethnic cleansing, like population control, some of our children will die at their own hands or that of a peer. We legislate that they remain children until they turn 18? Some childhood.

[JUNIOR COLLEGE, AGES 21-OPEN ENROLLMENT] Co-ed dorms and campuses put our daughters at risk. The elephant in the room is the barbaric and classless behavior between male and female going on behind closed doors. College needs to become more professional and civilized. Just like modeling school teaches young adults how to walk into a room, there need to be classes that teach young people how to conduct themselves in the public sector. Young ladies need to learn and get a strong conviction to stay sober in public places and when going solo to a party. AT ISSUE: CAMPUS SEXUAL VIOLENCE opens the introduction with this statement: "*Campus sexual violence is a very real problem, although there are many differing views about its prevalence, its causes, and the most effective ways of preventing it from occurring. What we do know for sure is that campus sexual violence affects many more women than men, that women may feel shame or fear in reporting a sexual attack that they experienced, and that many universities have historically tried to dissuade victims from contacting the police or going public with information about their attack....*"

University campuses need couples apartments, daycare centers, strict sexual harassment policies, elective classes that teach professional etiquette which will help College Graduates sit at a table with royalty. ALL OVER THE NATION COLLEGES NEED CLUBS THAT: (1) UNIFY DIFFERENT RELIGIONS

BY FOCUSING UPON WHAT THEY HAVE IN COMMON. (2) UNIFY AND DEBRIEF THE ANGER OF SLAVERY AND THE LOSSES OF THE CIVIL WAR. (3) HELP YOUNG WOMEN COME OUT OF THEIR SEXY KITTEN IMAGE OF FEMALE HETEROSEXUALITY. (4) HELP HETEROSEXUALS UNDERSTAND THE PROBLEMS OF LGBTQ FAMILY MEMBERS.

Teens should also be required to work their way through college, that would help. Easy financial aide has done a lot of damage to our economy. Millions of dollars are not going to products and services, but are recycling back into the U.S. Treasury from which it was borrowed. The Internet offers hope for future education at the University level. In Kevin Carey's <u>THE END OF COLLEGE</u>... he gives hope in his point of view concerning the future of a University education: *"At the University of Everywhere, educational resources that have been scarce and expensive for centuries will be abundant and free. Anything that can be digitized: books, lecture videos, images, sounds, and increasingly powerful digital learning environments; will be available to anyone in the world with an Internet connection."*

[TUTORING] Involvement. Even good students might enjoy the attention that ultimately will come from tutoring. The positive about tutoring is accountability. It will be difficult to run with a group of rebels when there is someone at home waiting to help with homework or studying for tests. Marina Ruben writes, in <u>HOW TO TUTOR YOUR OWN CHILD</u>, *"Princeton Review, Huntington Learning Center, Sylvan Learning Center, Kaplan Tutoring, SCORE—America is awash in tutoring companies. It's a $4 billion industry, and it seems as if every Helicopter Parent is buying in. If only there were a resource closer to home that was easy, free, and able to provide the same quality of service that students receive with an outside tutor. But there is: you."*

[HOME HIGH SCHOOL] We have the most free schooling of any country in the world, but a new form of oppression. Why can't this country get it right? Always a need to enslave, always a need to control. Why children? Children are the future and we are not all cut out the same way like a batch of cookies. Will parents ever again have control over their own children? When do good parents get to decide after watching their own child's response to public school that this is not beneficial to their child? Home school can be acquired by using internet and correspondence high school programs. Home school is a good alternative when a teen is emancipated and working a full time job. Also, sorry to say, in cases of bullying, being the bully, or dropping out. The internet and a self study program should parallel to the public school curriculum sufficiently. It is very important to make sure they get a real education through the Home School option. Home school should be a better choice and not a guarantee of substandard learning. Most children need the social part of school, but there are those who learn reading, writing and arithmetic better at home and away from the crowds. In this century we have internet education and correspondence schools so our home school children can get a quality education if they want it.

When a child enters high school parents need to pay close attention. If it looks like the child is over stressed or acting out, then it is time for a vacation. Home school needs to be for real, not another way to hide abused children. The school district needs to work with home school parents like they are teachers and request a copy of the year's syllabus. Parents must be required to give proof of a routine and learning goals of the children involved. Home school should be as much a copy of the public school curricula as possible, since the point of it is to be at home, not to be less educated. Thirteeners as emancipated adults should have rights to decide to stay home, or get a job, or go on to college, all alternatives to high school. There is the possibility that parents will force or threaten them to attend high school. With adult rights they can refuse, they can move out or leave home legally. That is not a desirable outcome, but there will always be bully parents. Having legal rights to leave home will solve some problems and help some lives.

[GENERAL DISCUSSION] We, The United States of America, force feed irrelevant facts and subjects to our children also known as intellectual "Junk Food" when all they need is basic reading, writing and arithmetic. Generally allow for reading a lot of books, magazines and newspapers and doing book reports. Teach them practical foreign languages that will help them get good paying jobs, like French, Spanish, German, Gaelic, Mandarin and Vietnamese. Introduce them to building construction, automotive, computer and small home repairs. There shouldn't be a grading scale on who is the smartest because bragging about being smarter than everybody is the worst social mistake of all.

Allow the boys and girls to do non-traditional classes in shop and cooking, playing sports and STEM classes. COMMON CORE is utter nonsense and child abuse. Learning needs to be fun. Children should be encouraged, rewarded, or paid to learn what they do not need or desire to learn. They should never be pressured, threatened or belittled. Let them have a one or two year break to decide about high school. If they find jobs, then going back to school is pretty much a waste of time. Our government should encourage teens to keep jobs by amending child labor laws so mature teens can work full-time in place of attending public education.

'Involving your children in resolving mechanical or maintenance problems in the house, such as unclogging a garbage disposal, fixing a broken toilet, mending a leaking faucet, changing a door knob, oiling a squeaky hinge, repairing a malfunctioning dishwasher, or painting a stained wall... If you want your children to become capable, self-sufficient, and fulfilled adults, you need to equip them with certain life skills that may not be taught in school Getting good grades alone does not guarantee success in life."
[from Chris Palmer, <u>RAISE</u> YOUR KIDS TO SUCCEED]

CHAPTER FOUR

CO-ED PUBLIC HIGH-SCHOOLS

*"It were better for him that a millstone were hanged about his neck
and he were cast into the sea, than that he should offend one of these
little ones" Luke 17:2*

Sure, you can get a college degree in anything you want with a photographic memory, but if you do not have a proper upbringing that comes from time with your family, it will be very hard to keep that career. High school has been destroying sensitive souls for decades. It is time to take a stand before we look up and there is no one qualified or sober enough to work a service job or run a grocery store. The greatest generation of World War II, left home at 13 years old, got married and worked full time jobs. They were not forced to act like children. They were not forced by truant officers to stay under submission of parents less educated, less intelligent, or less mature than themselves. They were allowed to shoulder the burden if their parents were sick or disabled. They did not have high school like it is today. The Bible was the main book in their curriculum. They pledged allegiance to our country's flag. They got consequences for criminal behavior. They put family and money making ahead of education, which is the right priority. They lived their religious beliefs and also prayed in school.

When did freedom loving Americans become sheep for the slaughter with the public education system? If we really want this nation to become great again then we will need to get uncomfortable and do the hard work and the necessary diligence that it will take. Why aren't parents fighting for high school to be more work oriented and to give college credit in every subject? How about separating the genders so sex won't happen so easily under the bleachers and in empty closets and Locked classrooms? Teens attending high school should be aiming for college because there is nothing new being learned here, it is all review. The basics have been covered a thousand times over: Phonetic Reading, Writing, English, Spelling and Algebra. Good high-schools need to be linked with a nearby community college. We are heading towards parental absenteeism at an exponential level.

The normal family of the future will have parents working long hours to "Keep up with the Kardashians." Children will have no other choice but to supervise themselves and spend long hours home alone. America has the power to make up its mind to help children survive their lives of poverty, abandonment and family crime. In high school, materialism is the focus, not self direction and purpose. Reading books and memorizing pages of words is not for everybody. It is a gift that not all people have. We are forcing children who love country music to listen to hours of opera music. We are frowning upon their love of country music and forcing the opera music upon them with the belief that without this opera music they will fail at life. Which is a big fat prevarication.

School is still a place full of strangers who do not know you or care about you. All they care about is their curriculum. They take control of your household. They tell you when and what to do. They will act like police officers and treat you like a criminal, all for outside the home activities that your child is not even getting paid for? NOT EVEN COLLEGE CREDIT? Parents are powerless and that should not be the case. Teachers deserve better salaries, but they do not deserve our worship and the souls of our children. So many of the poor are on government assistance and they do not have the basic social skills necessary for getting along with strangers in a job setting because of living in crime infested neighborhoods where socializing makes you vulnerable to attack.

Our co-ed public high schools are not training them for holding down jobs. They need to get grades in Social Skills: How to negotiate without losing one's temper. How to cooperate with someone else's rules. How to get in a line and wait patiently. How to just be quiet and observe in a public facility. How to look at your own bad behavior through someone else's eyes. As more and more of the teen-aged population become deeply entrenched in crime, drugs, pornography, shop-lifting, mail fraud and prostitution for fast money, providing a home for able-bodied young adults will become less and less a priority. More and more children will be wondering the streets at night waiting for the school doors to open up. The young people who choose to go to school to get on with a college education might need to escape a criminal or violent home life by living on a school campus. Dormitories and houses at the public high school level (not just universities and juvenile detention) should become normal in the 22nd century. High school has a life of its own and it is a controlling influence. Female stereotypes of behavior continue to be passed on to the next generation. Girls are cheerleaders, take Home Economics class and do not have ball games, wrestling, body-building or boxing classes. Boys have all the popular sports to join, wrestling, body-building, archery, sports and boxing. Homecoming King and Queen are always a couple and never solo in the 21st century, or two Kings, or two Queens.

Like a spirit of possession, high school takes control and parents cease to matter: family tree, bloodline, inheritance, your own last name, it all gets sucked into a psychological sink hole. High school ravages a virgin's religious beliefs and consumes the soul much like serving in the military, because co-ed high school, like co-ed military service, is really a man's world. The emotions will go away and the young people will be stronger and smarter, super adults who never fall in love and give away their lives and their dreams for other human beings, like a spouse or children. The evidence and witnesses makes it appear that the alleged ultimate goal of the American education system is to control natural affection and population. America's young women turn 18 and go into the job market unmarried with some sexual experience; a vast majority of them are single and childless.

Co-Ed Public High Schools teach all about condoms, pills and cycle techniques to stop teen girls from getting pregnant, a natural consequence of sexual intercourse. This truant system forces girls out of the house and into classrooms full of horny boys and old men. Then they are trained to walk down the street all alone and through back alleys, if they don't catch a ride after school. What is wrong with that picture? Men are not there for them. Men are not watching over them to protect them. Yet they live for men's attention. They dream all day that a man will love them. They wear skimpy attire to get men to lust upon their bodies, not their brains. They do not want men to know how smart they really are. When they were 13 they had a different attitude. They had more self awareness and caution and they let their brains show. Every sex education class should include basic instructions for taking care of babies and small children. Bring a real live baby to the class with its teen mom. Why? So the young people will be motivated to use the birth control devices; make it real, not just another boring lecture. Today's high schools facilitate a lot of sneakiness to have illegal and forbidden sex.

You should be sure if your son or daughter can survive high school, if you have a doubt, better examine why you have your doubts. Do not put your child in the fire, do not sacrifice your child to the "God Of Materialism," who will chew them up, spit them out and leave them in a ditch to die. The Board of Education says… "We do not want teen marriages or pregnancies, but teen promiscuity is okay as long as it is not prostitution. Sex should be for fun and sport, not for married couples only. So just get over that abortion and statutory rape. You are too young to care about morality, God's will, or your future." Why are good Christian parents tolerating secular philosophies about teens and sex?

Sex is not a sport. A child who is having sex no matter what people say has already lost innocence and purity. Sexual teens infect nonsexual teens. No wonder teen pregnancy looks like an epidemic. Today's Co-Ed Public High Schools are becoming more like brothels and drug houses. There are teachers and parents looking the other way while their teenagers facilitate a lot of sneaking around to have sex, smoke marijuana, pop over-the-counter pills, give blow jobs and hide from violent parents and law enforcement.

Socializing and engaging in the immediate family goes down the toilet because of all the studying and memorizing of useless information that will never be called upon to live a successful and happy life. The Co-Ed Public high school system does not seem to be producing hard working and well behaved employees. If the school system were a person it would be charged with child abuse and corruption of minors. Is it a "defacto" conspiracy to produce a babyish and deflowered population of poor young adults with low morals and low self esteem, over and over and over again? "What a despicable use of tax dollars!" Excessive education without a purpose has been interfering with the growth and development of America's young people for decades now.

High school encourages foolish and childish behavior. The wholesome life of a 13 year old girl dries up and blows away once she sets her foot inside a high school. This is where 13 as the adult age will protect the child. Parents can be an active part of picking out a suitable match for their son or daughter, not the local high school. It will also be easier for young people to maintain sexual purity if they have a legal right to just say "NO!" to high school. If high schools were human beings, they would be charged with child abuse. Excessive unnecessary education is destroying the teenagers of the USA by manipulating them into satisfying their sexual needs with immoral and antisocial behaviors. Marriage is completely discouraged. The "Too Young" excuse, but nothing is done to discourage sex; all the branches of the high school tree point towards it.

This type of lawmaking is from people who do not read the Holy Bible. I believe lawmakers see high school as a great invention, a gift to young people, a way of saying "Stay children for as long as possible because being an adult really sucks." America's high school system is like a pedophile delinquent friend who seduces teenagers into enjoying forbidden sex, but offers no good advice for when they get caught. The average American parent cannot control their 13 year old child who is the size of a full grown adult, but the law expects them to control that child to the age of 18. Every home in America with a teenager has a power struggle going on. A tug of war between a teenager and his or her parent. All the teenager wants is to be an adult. All the parent wants is to control this child from doing something stupid. Nobody wins. We are not thinking, we are not being human, we are not serving God. Our daughters should not be forced to go to places without bodyguards and chaperones where they can get kidnapped, raped, or seduced into consensual intercourse. There is no heart and soul in the public high school education system of today, but we expect the young people to turn out normal and moral. In this freedom minded country in which women and girls are on their own to survive, we still have girly girls and sex kittens as role models to our hurt. Going against nature and God expecting "good" results is a fool's game. Can anyone go against God and win?

We have millions of lost and lonely souls in America today. So you went to high school and became promiscuous to fit in and now you are condemned to a lifetime of loneliness and desperation. How is that a good thing? The guilt and shame of what they did behind their parents' backs that exceeds a simple sin of fornication is why they drink too much and need to stay mentally numb. Why were they denied teen marriage with their first love experience? What was more important than love? Controlling the population? A high school diploma? College? Football? We keep holding young people back and the schools keep using books and traditions that are over 100 years old. This type of lawmaking shows how we need Bibles in the educational system because this kind of legislation goes against God and natural human laws.

Co-ed public high schools thumb up their noses towards Heaven and say to God, "We will do it our way, not nature's way or God's way. What God joins together we will most definitely pull apart." High school is the most unnatural environment your children will ever experience. It is for mating, plain and simple. It is no different than being in a herd or a flock, but animals are okay to mate. The morally weak of high school who get pregnant and marry will be frowned upon. If they get saddled with a baby, they are likely to stay poor for all their lives. Not because they were too young but because they were not prepared for independence and child rearing, and once the baby is born they get a decade behind in financial security. Especially with their parents refusing to help them survive. Wanting the baby to go up for adoption and scolding them for not getting an abortion. The morally strong ones will develop a sense of fear towards marriage and child rearing. Many of them will remain childless until the biological clock sounds an alarm. Not all the blame is at the parenting level because the children are also being raised by their teachers as well. Teachers are co-parenting all the time, for better or for worse. The disrespect they give their parents they will give their teachers, the respect they give their parents will be given to the teacher also. The normal parental hate and love as well.

Make high school more like a corporation and the students more like employees. If they have a gift or talent they could be using to support their family, like singing, writing, sports or art, allow them to make money from it. All of this education is supposed to be for a purpose, the untalented and ungifted will need college degrees. Gifted and talented should escape the grip of forced learning and move on with their lives. High School should not be holding gifted and talented young adults back from being successful in life. Upgrading high schools and expecting more of 8th grade graduates will ultimately help America become great again. I hope and pray that the 50% who agree with me will attempt to do something about it. Don't be passive anymore about your child's future. Today's Co-Ed Public high schools are hindrances to spiritual and emotional growth. This letter is not against middle school, it is against the average Co-Ed Public high school. Co-Ed Public high school is not for everybody.

Many young people are done with school by the age of 13. Advanced education needs to be a choice connected to a nearby community college. Now as a compromise, there could be specialty schools. These schools should have unisex uniforms that are an everyday part of the young people's wardrobe, like jeans, running shoes, T-shirts and vests. They should have the routine of clocking in and out and bringing their own sack lunch, but lockers should have transparent fiberglass doors for security reasons. Co-Ed Public high schools need to be work oriented and for career preparation.

Athletes, cheer-leaders and band students benefit most from attending Co-Ed Public high school. They are the happiest of the students because they get worshiped and envied. They also get a lot of friends and go on a lot of dates. No other group of children get more positive attention, worship and admiration through four years of high school and beyond. These young people have the best times of their lives. They have memories to hold them through the tough times of adulthood and parenting the next generation while they work at boring jobs that do not provide enough income to own a lightly used car in the capital cities of "Broken Dreams" "False Promises," and "Birds Rising From Ashes" all over the USA.

Of course there are people who want Co-Ed Public High School with all of its bells and whistles for their teenagers. They want sports, cheerleaders, band and the "promenade" dance. They should make money from tickets to their ball games. Also, they should be given college credit. They should clock in and out of their classrooms and any sexual misconduct or bullying should be addressed as a crime. A court system should be set up at the school so children will use a nonviolent problem solving practice as a learning experience. There should be a social hour to teach social skills since most of the poor children never go anywhere. They never sit at a table, except for Thanksgiving, where there are different silverware and napkins. They will need the school to help them learn how to do small talk, the importance of an inside voice, the importance of a public personality to get along with strangers and the ability to overlook rude behavior.

Students and teachers should be conforming to dress codes. Students should clock in and out to keep up with attendance. Create a token economy for good behavior, arriving five minutes early and perfect attendance. Keep grades and teacher comments confidential, no public announcements to the whole school of how well a child is doing. Jealousy should not be encouraged or desired. They should have sexual harassment classes and be subject to legal action if they assault someone. Unless the school is run by a church, there should be a legitimate government flavor to the school. Like a childcentric society ought to feel. There should be allegiance to the flag and entry level job recruiters.

There should also be a code of conduct for boys and girls that encourages respect. If a boy misbehaves he is taken away from co-ed classes, and placed in the all boy classroom for the rest of that semester. There should also be daycare centers at every high school. The high school of the future should have the following attributes: Quiet, under control, conservative attire, clock in and out like a job, bring your own lunch, misbehavior not tolerated, strict sexual harassment rules with nearby childcare centers and baby nurseries. Grades need to be private and confidential. The learning atmosphere will be non-competitive, nonviolent, non-racist, non-homophobic, nonsexist and non-xenophobic. Teens have the choice of all boy or all girl classrooms. Asking too much? I do not believe it is.

Co-Ed Public High Schools need to become sanctuaries for victims of sexual abuse and rape. There needs to be a direct connection to task forces with surveillance capability so that child victims will have the confidence to come forward. We don't need to tolerate child predators becoming lawyers and judges and giving slaps on the wrist to their own kind in this century. Co-Ed Public High Schools should produce law abiding citizens, if not, then they need a total overhaul of their curriculum. Perhaps public high schools should be military and professional. Perhaps there should be three public school models to suit the kind of students that they serve. Wealthy neighborhoods could have a performing arts with sports model, middle income could have a military leadership training model, and poverty neighborhoods a police academy model for obvious reasons.

Maybe if Co-Ed Public high schools could be sued for how dangerous and negligent they are with the well being of our children the government would listen to parent and teacher complaints. Chronic study leads to promiscuity. The brain is so strong from constantly memorizing that the thought of doing sex will lead to sex. If you break weak and start dating with the idea you will be careful, you won't be a virgin on your wedding night. A way to make high school more useful and practical for all young people is to pay young people for attending high school and learning stuff they did not choose for themselves. Of course, it is the poor who are suffering the most from these age limit laws. Rich kids and middle class hardly feel the pressures of a family needing all hands on deck to pay the rent and put food on the table. Today's high schools with poor children should give coupons and cash for good grades, attendance and good behavior. The teens could exchange the coupons at any participating store for the basic needs of food, clothes, bus passes and school supplies. That would help the financial burden of their unemployed or minimum wage earning parents. It could also curtail dropping out. Because, no doubt, there are young people who are dropping out of high school and working the maximum hours allowable at a fast food restaurant or a landscaping job to help their single parent.

[LGBTQ TEENAGERS] The church should be evangelizing the LGBTQ community, since some teens born and raised in church will turn out to be lesbian, gay, bisexual, transgender or question-mark. Maybe God Our Creator has placed LGBTQ children in this world to show us how bad it is to put boys and girls together daily for 5 days a week, from age 2 to 18, without anyone being encouraged to see anyone of the opposite gender as marriage material. High School is not a wonderful place for the millions of young people who are trans or bi-gender. It might be a place to get murdered or brutally beaten simply for looking, acting or dressing a certain way. A place that is frightening and often violent. All acts of hazing and violence should be turned over to the police, not swept under the rug.

Teens of the LGBTQ community will best move forward during these awful years with their own separate charter high schools. They are similar to special kids with special needs because we as a society are refusing to evolve in our attitudes and blaming it on religion. In cases of verbal abuse and intimidation, the offended student could file a formal complaint against the bully and have a student council court hearing. Random students could be selected to participate as jurors and judges, and the plaintiff and defendant should represent themselves, produce evidence and argue their cases as an alternative to violence and grudge holding. A suitable punishment could be attending classes and doing the work, but not receiving grades for the work turned in. It would he a type of "Gender Therapy" if gender disabled teenagers were purposely put in gender separated classrooms. "Tomboys" with boys and "Girly Boys" with girls. This immersion increases opportunities for normal attractions to the opposite gender and helps them develop lasting friendships with the gender that is not afraid of them.

If this is a developmental phase it could begin to extinguish itself as the child has difficulty keeping up with the opposite gender. Or it will help the child have a sense of belonging, so either way, it will be a positive environment for Lesbian, Gay and Transgender teenagers, unlike the movie, <u>BOY ERASED.</u> Also, it is a known fact that the same gender is absolutely petrified with fear of homosexuals. This puts Lesbian girls and Gay boys in danger of being verbally abused and seriously hurt in a heterosexual high school. Scared adults are dangerous and scared teenagers are even more so, united with their parents. Courage classes and self-esteem classes should be taught in public high-school, but not very likely to occur in my lifetime, that would be much too futuristic and logical.

CHAPTER FIVE

SECRETS OF TEENS

"For God will bring every work into judgment, with every secret thing, whether it be good, or whether it be evil." Ecclesiastes 12:14

Villi and Mary Kay, a teacher and a 13 year-old had a secret love affair that was blown out of proportion by the media and the courts. Wasted litigation and wasted money in the Correctional system. God Almighty cannot legislate who we can love once the age of 13 takes full effect. Villi and Mary Kay should not have been prosecuted, they should have been counseled. Now more thirteeners than ever before will have gone into hiding. The public humiliation created more problems than it was designed to deter. No reporters seemed to care that Villi suffered from depression at the negative press, and his love for Mary Kay did not go away like a schoolboy crush was supposed to.

Who, America, do we think we are? Here is a young man with an extra serving of male hormones and sexual experience who pursued a full grown woman in a manly way and got her. This should have been kept private. I repeat, 13 years is long enough to be treated as a child. That does not mean abuse them, but it means give them rights and authority over their own lives within the guidelines of morality, religion, common sense and safety. We want to change nature in this country. We nationally castigated a consensual attraction between a 13 year-old and a full grown woman which culminated into a committed marriage. It is too late to go backwards. A 13 year-old child living like an adult can only go forwards. He was a student and she was still legally married. Counseling makes a lot more sense and is more compassionate than separation and jail time. This woman was unfairly incarcerated and labeled a pedophile sex predator. They gave birth to two beautiful girls and raised them well. We, this society of legal ageism, put a stigma on their love that made it extra difficult. No loving union should go through that.

In a Black teen coming-of-age movie, "THE WOOD", at 13 years old three young men made a decision to never get married, just go for the sex. They even make a bet about it. It ends with one of them getting married, 13 years later, to his first true love. No one was a virgin bride. Education was the number one priority to being alive in their teens. All human emotions and deep feelings for teen aged girls had to be put on hold. They obeyed the law against young people getting married, but sex was okay, as long as they didn't get caught. They all went to college and searched for job security, the one who got married did not have a job as good as his future bride's, but he had lots of baggage from fooling around from bedroom to bedroom. The guilt and fear dominated the story as his best friends sobered and cleaned him up so he would not jilt his bride. The ultimate goal in their lives had been colored with the shade of shame due to a lot of secret make-out sessions and quick forbidden sex behind their parents' backs. All three of them felt undeserving of real love and a happy marriage.

So-called "Good Teens" have dirty little secrets hard to hide forever. God has put hormones in their bodies and we expect them to succeed where their parents have failed in a sexcentric environment and society at large. We read in the Bible to "flee fornication" while we dress our daughters like hookers and put them in every classroom with horny, sexually deprived teen boys and male teachers who probably read Playboy and Hustler. So-called "Good kids" will go underground with their sex lives. Worse than that, these grown ups we keep calling "Children" have no goals, jobs, or purpose for living; and you wonder why they turn violent, run away from home, get addicted to drugs and alcohol, commit acts of rape, molestation and sexual promiscuity.

We keep our children as children to their hurt and ours as well. Now sexual relations between adults and 13 year olds has gone underground and in many cases it gets paid for. So the child becomes a prostitute, not a wife or mother, an intelligent "Lolita" sleeping with teachers for good grades. A best kept secret and a reason for drinks and drugs. This is why running away from home needs to be decriminalized. There is no better and louder way to cry for help To leave home with no destination, walking the streets and refusing to set foot inside your own home with your flesh and blood parents, who is that hurting? We have an over reaching government that puts young adults in position to be brutalized, tortured, raped or killed by their own parents. Who in their right mind wants to go out in the streets at night without a warm bath, a warm clean bed to sleep on and a good meal to eat? Who would run away from home for nothing or because everything is nurturing and secure?

A sex life is pretty much a reason for moving out of the house. Do not hate your child for not exceeding your DNA, but help your child put a life together. Do not destroy the parent child friendship over your child being human. Yes, your child has secrets. There are incidents that your children have survived and do not ever want to discuss, never, not even on the day they die. There should be no shame at knowing that 13 is an age to become sexually active. Mother Nature will force the issue upon young people no matter how well raised they may be. Marriage will save them from shame and bad sexual encounters that lead to sexual obsession. It is more immoral to avoid marriage. Young people are having sex parties where boys line up and girls give them blow jobs. So instead of marrying and raising children with mom and dad's assistance, young people are going to a dark side and living a secret, immoral, sex life.

Do a good job teaching them right from wrong and social skills for those first 13 years. Teach them to just say no to adults touching them in a sexual way, make a call or write a letter, do something to turn such adults in. Most 13 year olds have high moral values if they are not pushed and prodded into an immoral lifestyle. Even a transgender teen might not follow through on those disturbing attractions, might make a decision to give heterosexuality a chance, taking a stand to try to be normal first. Society's 13 year olds are afraid to assert their true feelings and hide it from his or her parents. They often hold back feelings about wanting to put high school on hold and work a full time job that is legal and easy to excel at. We need to change child labor laws so 13 year olds will be allowed to take on adult responsibilities and work full-time, light labor jobs, such as computer techs, receptionists, fast food restaurants, or whatever they are physically and mentally capable of doing. Moving out one day, getting into a serious and committed relationship one day, should not be a secret. They need to feel that growing up is okay with mom and dad and they don't need to keep their truth a deep, dark secret.

Being kept by their parents like a small child needing pampering and supervising only creates a sense of shame and guilt in the soul realm. Also, a sense of self destruction that often leads to a lifetime of medications, poverty, bad choices and sadness. All they do is go behind their parents' backs, or run away from home to live another life under another name. Does anyone care?

CHAPTER SIX

ADOPTION OPTION

"For you did not receive the spirit of bondage again to fear, but you received the Spirit of Adoption by whom we cry out, Abba, Father."
Romans 8:15

On Sunday night there was a TV show on channel 40 titled, *Long Lost Family*. Over and over there is this scenario of young love that led to a normal and natural response between two young people. In another country they would have been married. How dare America see their way as better. Giving up babies for adoption when the parents are alive and healthy is not a better way. Make sure you date only the people you dream of having sex with. Do not be a user, because users get used. The desires start at age 13, expecting to escape sex traps until age 18 is very unrealistic. Moral failure is sure to happen, will you get an abortion to cover it up or give a baby away like a kitten or puppy? Remember that you are not getting younger, you are getting older, does that help you make a decision?

Abortion and adoption is not the answer for young people, it just complicates their spiritual walk. A lot of them never get over the psychological repercussions of losing their virginity before marriage and getting a "secret abortion." Unchaperoned Dating, an American invention, frequently leads to casual sex or date rape, which frequently leads to a pregnancy. In the book, *BARE MINIMUM PARENTING.* James Breakwell comes up with some real good points about teen parenting: *"If you have a baby before you can legally vote, there's a 99 percent chance it was a mistake.... If you procreate in your teenage years and you still live at home, there's a chance your parents will raise the kid for you...."*

Adoption should not be an option, that is your blood relative, you need to reject all thoughts of giving a baby away just because your teens are not prepared, because they can get prepared. A temporary foster care arrangement is all that is necessary.

All teenagers will become adults if they keep on living. America should give all young people in every state the right to marry as an option to abortion and adoption. Allow them to put a child in temporary foster care while they get their lives in order, being too young is temporary. Give them the choice to raise their own flesh and blood and to be in their first baby's life. Limit the adoption option to situations that are worse than being too young. America think about what you are doing to family trees. What has happened to our country? Why do we throw babies away so easily, whether in the womb or out of it? Abortion continues being legal into the 3rd trimester so babies can be killed for non-health related reasons. This is a self-destructive normal for our country, a self-appointed form of voluntary genocide.

When will this country wake up to its own perversion of family values and God's purpose for fertility? Babies are supposed to be blessings, a new member, a replacement, a continuation of a family's bloodline, and we throw that away with abortions and giving up babies for adoption for no other excuse than "too young." I will say what others have refused to say because I have no political party to impress. We are creating our own genocide and destroying our own race and family tree. It is wrong to give away babies because you are not ready, it is wrong to abort a perfectly healthy fetus and walk away like it was nothing. You did not have a funeral, did not create a birth/death certificate, just walked away like it was nothing, was it a glob of cells? What did your heart say?

It is like parents are under some kind of hypnotic spell to give up unplanned babies. Only the planned babies deserve to stay or live. They do not care what the teens want to do about it. They see it is as a consequence for bad behavior and they are blind to the greater wrong of giving the newborn away. Were they too young to take on the responsibility of raising their own creation? The state of being an underage teenager is a temporary problem. Actually their parents were too uncaring, plain and simple. God bless them, we are all in a spiritual and moral fog making commandments of men a standard for raising our children. Stop being so quick to give up newborn babies for adoption just because the parents are not seen as adults.

I am not interested in changing adoption legislation when the best fix is giving young people the rights of adulthood before engaging in the sex that God designed them to have. The parents should have seen it from a mile away. Very few teenagers do not have those feelings for the opposite gender. Dating should not be engaged in if the teen is not prepared for mating. Parents could invite the attractive friend over for dinner or family outings. On the other hand, if the young man or woman is interested in dating, then he or she should be encouraged to prepare for mating. There needs to be a focused determination to finish high-school as early as possible, get an entry level job with benefits and chance for promotion, save money to move into an apartment. Learn how to drive in order to lease a gas-saving economy car. College will always be there, but the chance for love and family might come once in a lifetime. Abortion is not always the choice young people make. When aborting a pregnancy does not lead to killing a fetus, and the time is soon coming, then fetuses will be put up for adoption.

Adoption should be for when one or both parents are suspected child molesters, have died, are incarcerated, working in a sex career, undocumented, terminally ill or much too mentally deficient through drugs, alcohol or a very low IQ. The baby could have been put in a foster home until the "baby parents" get their lives together. Babies having babies is normal, inconvenient and uncomfortable, but not a sin or a crime. We are not put on this planet to stay babies forever. Being fruitful and multiplying comes naturally and it is a gift from almighty God, not something to be ashamed of or hidden under the proverbial carpet.

CHAPTER SEVEN

TEEN VIRGINITY

"Nevertheless he who stands steadfast in his heart, having no necessity, but has power over his own will, and has so determined in his heart that he will keep his virgin, does well." 1 Corinthians 7:37

NO VIRGINITY=NO MARRIAGE! In The Bible, Tamar begged her half-brother, Amnon, not to rape her. If he truly loved her, he would have yielded to her pleas. He thought having sex without commitment would make him happy and he likely wanted her to be that kind of girl, but she was a Kingdom girl. Her half-brother's day of giving in to lust destroyed her future and her hope of marital happiness. Her father, King David, was criticized by another brother, Absalom, for not stepping up to the plate and making things right for his daughter. King David may have been conflicted about defending Tamar because by rule of law, if he killed Amnon for being a rapist, then he also needed to kill Tamar for being a rape victim. She did not put up a fight or scream so the servants would come in to rescue her. Lots of rape victims freeze with fear, but screaming was a legal requirement to keep a rape from looking like consent. Tamar's child was born out of wedlock and that was shameful back then. Forty centuries later it is still a shame to be born out of wedlock as a consequence of first love passion or statutory rape.

In Bible days, even if a girl said it was not with her consent, she was forced to marry a man accused of forcing her to have sex with him, because every baby born needed to be born in wedlock in this society set aside by God. Also, in that culture, parents could not marry off a daughter who had lost her virginity. Obviously, marriage was for a girl's survival or to maintain her moral reputation. Virginity also gave a girl or woman moral value. To lose virginity and not get married immediately afterwards was devastating. The man who would rape a girl or woman and refuse to marry her, had to have been looked upon as disgusting in God's eyes. We have come a long way under God's Grace, we have so much mercy and kindness that we literally encourage sex outside of marriage. We literally encourage virgins to refuse to marry.

It is not that easy to get love. Love might not come around again. Love is really the glue of life, so look at marriage, or a long engagement to get married at 18, if that will satisfy everyone involved, but you will likely have a baby out of wedlock, so be faithful to that one person, boy or girl. That is my advice to you. In our country virginity is the enemy, so we make sure no one stays a virgin. Do not even give them a chance to consider remaining a virgin for life. All of America's young people are pushed to have illicit sex for the experience alone by sex education classes focused upon birth control methods. So by the time they turn 18 they only need the opposite sex for sexual pleasure, but not for love, seems to be the agenda. Promiscuity is not the answer. Look at the insanity, look at the kidnappings, look at the rapes, hear the stories about incest and child prostitution. The money made from pornography exceeds the national debt. All from a nation that scoffs at virginity and the concept of virgin teen brides.

Sexless dating is wonderful and most virgins can pull it off until their hormones take control. We are not all the same with our hormone clocks. If you love God, drop promiscuity like a hot rock. Promiscuity is not a problem-solving skill. Save your sex for a real relationship based upon what you have in common and a strong physical attraction with the blessing of your family. Consider a long engagement, love takes time, unlike lust, love is a process. Stop listening to the excuse YOU ARE TOO YOUNG. You will regret it. Celibacy is not the end of the world, but we have created so much glory around sexual intercourse that children who should not be wanting to experience sex are wanting to have sex lives: Autistic and Asperger's Syndrome, Down's and some LGBTQ kids are happiest in a sex free world. The school system keeps them sexually aroused while telling them they cannot do anything about it until they turn 18. If they could just have a choice, they could live happier lives. Happy people make good choices and treat people right.

There is a strong consensus that the Virgin Mary was pregnant with The Son of God at 13 years-old. Even if Mary the Mother of Jesus Christ was impregnated by the Holy Spirit, (Immaculate Conception of course) on her 13th birthday (which makes perfect sense knowing God) she would have been 13 and 9 months old when her child, The Savior of the World, was born. In numerology 13 and 9 are very special numbers. The Bar Mitvah and Bath Mitzvah were customary in Jewish tradition that at the age of 13 young people were seen as adults in training. Falling back on that fact, it is not a stretch to see God use a 13 year-old virgin girl to carry His Son, Jesus Christ. This is all speculation, but two points are agreed upon by Bible historians, Mary was under 18, and Mary was a virgin.

When we graduated from elementary school most of us kept on being our naturally good selves, our Christian selves. Most of us did not throw off our shackles of childhood and defy our parents rules and leave home without a plan. Hypothetically, don't expect every 13-year old girl to jump into marriage, some are lesbian, transgender or bisexual. It would be nice to be able to come out of the closet concerning sex at age 13.

In lots of religious cultures virginity is a normal standard. Middle Eastern teen girls are not pushed and prodded to dress sexy and go on two-person dates. They are not given the responsibility of controlling men who are drawn to them. On the contrary, they are over-dressed and over-supervised on a constant and daily basis, and they are chaperoned often with a male relative when walking around the community. They are taught to date in groups and not to be walking places all alone, or meeting that love interest all alone. They involve their parents, they do not jump the broom with perfect strangers off the Internet.

VIRGINITY was a part of the definition of marriage in the Old Testament. A portion of this thought is in The Book of Deuteronomy, chapter 22, verses 13-21. Virginity was part of the definition of marriage, if a man could prove his wife was not a virgin, he could throw her out of the house and let the neighbors stone her death. They called sex before marriage an evil thing, not to be tolerated, punishable by death. Without stating a specific age, that culture emphasized that female virgins do not date but wait on their parents to choose them a husband. Even a virgin young man could have been given in marriage to an older young woman, as in Genesis, chapter 38, verses 6-11. Of course the young people had the right to protest, but most trusted in their parent's judgment. So parents played a strong role in selecting mates for their virgin teens: Not the government and not "Random Chance." In Bible times whoever you had sex with you had to marry that person. That is why a rapist had to marry the victim according to law. Whoever you had sexual penetration with was by law, designated to become your husband or wife, whether you wanted that person or not. The prolonging of adulthood rights gives too much time to develop immorality as a social skill.

Teens need the choice to quit school and go to work. Maybe marry that one heterosexual person he or she feels an attraction to. They are forced to suck it up and go to high school and take a deep breath every morning until they finally graduate. Then here comes college, turning 18 means nothing, they are still being children, still putting off life for education in the hope of getting a job that is really just a dream, that might come true, no guarantees. Prerogatives will make life more worth living. Marriage is not the only reason to give adulthood to a 13 year old, the calling of God to go to Bible college, or finding a summer job that has a future. Bringing the family out of poverty, survival, unless of course high school will pay the rent; when athletes (other performing arts and spelling bee winners) draw a salary.

Poor girls do not have the hope and resources that middle class girls have. A poor girl needs to get a head start on working at a job and going to college, or finding a good man to get married to while she is a virgin. Incest victims can see themselves as virgins, because rape is not consensual. A man is using his daughter's body like she is not even a human being. He should buy himself an anatomically correct manikin and stop abusing his daughter. Ending childhood at 13 could help save a girl from incest rape. Virginity can be a wonderful gift on that wedding night. The future of high school for the poor is very shaky. What goes on in public high schools today would be rated 'X' if it were in a movie.

Most public high schools with a large poverty population are dangerous for virgins. Sexual arousal without a moral solution leads to predatory behavior and immoral choices of desperation. Parents in America seem to ignore their children's needs for love, and smarter nations are prepared for teen infatuations that often lead to unwanted pregnancies.

America balks at reporting Sexual Harassment. Besides date rape, teacher seduction, parental incest, street kidnappers and internet predators, America's teenagers do not have a safe choice for their lonely hearts. A lot of American 13 year olds have had a few "consensual" sexual encounters. Even if they were not caught because of birth control pills taken properly, or good contraceptive practices, they have self-loathing for giving away virginity without a fight. Look at the sexism in everyday fashion. Refuse to perpetuate the inequality of clothes and tailoring in which virgin little girls are forced to tolerate skimpy clothing and shoes their entire childhoods. They show more of their bodies than boys do as young as 2 years old. In Bible times virgins covered themselves, and nakedness, shaved head and bare feet was a punishment for haughtiness. We have come such a long way from when people cared about virginity. As a society and culture, we simply thumb up our noses at virginity. We need to get back to the basics and dress our VIRGINS like they are not for sex. Then we need to take sex out of the school. Separate classes for boys and girls.

Change sex education classes into family dynamics education, so that a baby is not looked upon as an unwanted object, or an undesirable outcome. Give them the answer to the question of "where do babies come from?" with a child-development class and some parenting basics. Help them make decisions concerning their first sexual experience that will make sense to the bigger picture of becoming responsible adults who don't depend upon their parents to bail them out of their sexual screw ups. Virginity until marriage would save many homosexuals and lesbians from AIDS, STD's, prostitution and abortion addiction. There is much guilt in the soul and a sense of self-hatred that often leads to a lifetime of depression. Does anyone care? Respect virginity: keep the sex-talk, dirty pictures and pornography, out of the classroom. There are high paying government jobs that will only hire virgins, no matter how smart or qualified you may be. Very few "sex starved" teenagers can stop themselves from having sex with someone they are strongly attracted to, as soon as possible.

CHAPTER EIGHT

TEEN MARRIAGE

"Whoever finds a wife, finds a good thing and obtains favor of the Lord." Proverbs 18:22

An episode of the TV show, "Guardian" showed pretty much what I am writing this book for. Two runaways, boy and girl, under legal age, caught up in the system with a newborn baby are given a chance to get their lives on track for their baby. The judge grants them emancipation, they are allowed to get married, they are allowed to work a job and they are allowed to live away from their parents. They are also given custody of their baby. Happy ending. No one should be judged by someone else's failure.

Marriage is a lot more normal than promiscuity. Most human beings, created to be like God, fall in love. Marriage seems to be made for men. Heterosexual men seem to need that one girl for a lifetime. We know our children will not contain their sexual drives. We stop them from working and contributing to the family income and we stop them from getting married while they are still virgins. We have ceased to live by God's natural laws while calling ourselves a CHRISTIAN NATION. Sexual unnaturalness is helping to destroy America, when marriage is a God ordained stabilizer that helps teenagers stop searching for Mr./Mrs. Right. The teen can focus on his or her life in the moment.

They will not have the stress of sneaking around behind their parents' backs to be with someone. It would impact this current new normal of "lonely" in teen years if 13ers had the right to marry for love, sexual expression and to create the next generation of their family tree. Teen boys seem to fall into insanity over a small amount of sexual arousal with a teen girl. The teen girl who does not fall in love with the young man puts her life and safety at risk, so out of fear, not attraction, she will date the young man. In America, boys have been known to murder girls who want to break up with them. Where are the parents? Parents do not seem to know their authority when it comes to supervising sexually active teenagers.

We are disrespecting God's time-table for being fruitful and multiplying. We want our own way and our children are suffering for it. Without legal adulthood, sex is the only reason for teen dating because marriage is out of reach. This is a reason for anger and rebellion. They are ready to move out and live on their own but the law and their parents keep suppressing their efforts to do things righteously, so they sneak around, lie to their parents, and do desperate things, all "for love, not sex," they will say.

All the choices of young women need to be celebrated. Not all females are meant to be married and those that choose against marriage should be given the same acceptance as those who are lucky at love. I would like emancipated 13 year old girls to work jobs that will help support themselves. They should not be looking for a man or woman with money to take care of them. Money cannot buy compatibility, nonviolence and faithfulness. Do not jump into bed with every person who thinks they love you. God's way: saving your sex for your wedding night will work out to be the best idea.

Dating around probably means that no one is likely to walk that aisle deserving of a white dress and a veil. After 13, the ability to hold back sexually decreases, if a girl is not kept busy, like actress Tamera Mowry, she is likely to seek a sexual experience. God gave us these drives and hormones that kick in at a certain age, an age of growing into an adult. We need our parents to protect us from bad judgments, but we also need to be recognized as ready for adult living and responsibilities. When we are detoured from sanity and common sense, we become hot messes. The poor and at risk teenagers, ages 13 to 17, need the right to marry without parental consent, the right to vote and the right to work full time and postpone high school. The fruit of this age-18 law is speaking loudly in crime rates and immorality. It is a lie to say that girls are better off kept as children until the age of 18. There are news stories almost everyday about girls who attract immature and violent young men that cannot allow them to break up with them. With parental supervision being mandatory towards a 13 year old adolescent it will potentially improve family unity and gene pool to get to know who is wanting to go steady with your child. If that person proves to be a horrible match it will be easier to influence and redirect a 13 year old, rather than an 18 year old.

The Apostle Timothy says that, in the last days people will forbid their children to marry. Pushing adulthood 5 years beyond what a human being needs can complicate a human being's life. God wants us to keep it simple. God's way is so simple, but it is not easy. Parents need to guide and counsel, not push their kids around like ogres and bulls do. Young people need to go to a full time job, learn how to drive a car, make plans well in advance for marriage and raising a baby. Birth control can be for newlywed teenagers. They need to plan their pregnancies more than any other age group while they are still getting ready and everything is new to them. Sex always brings some stress. The stress of a married couple working together is more positive and uplifting than the stress of a boy and girl sneaking around in the dark trying to avoid a scandal. Teen wives in America would do better than their sisters in 3rd World nations who are acquainted with arranged marriages. We have rights and laws already in place for our children's protection. In the case of 13 year olds getting married for love, who they marry is important. They should not marry people with criminal history, not violent people and not old people. The judge or magistrate marriage license representative should counsel them to make sure love and attraction is bringing this couple together, not money problems and desperation.

Make them abstain from premarital sex by keeping them chaperoned on dates. Some teens are very mature for their age. I am referring to ordinary people not millionaire celebrities. There is also a double standard for rich kids and celebrities. They are exempted from the legal age laws. They work fulltime jobs and make millions per year. They often have early sex lives, smoke, drink, do drugs and marry while under the age of 18. In other words, for the right price, they pay to be fully human between 13 and 18, and no one hollers "Foul!" One of the greatest singers, Celine Dion, married until death of a spouse, was married at 13. Jerry Lee Lewis and Elvis Presley married 13 year olds and those marriages lasted a very long time. There was also a 13 year old queen of France who was in the wrong place at the wrong time, but who cared so much about the poor that she offered them cake and pastries from her own table. No complaints from the ones who married at age 13. It is the unmarried promiscuous ones who waited until they were 18 to start living.

The girls should not be forced or threatened to marry men older than 18 that there is no attraction to or common ground with. No, not because he can provide for her the basics of rent, food, clothing, transportation, entertainment, recreation and provide for a baby. Love needs to be the primary reason for getting married. A young lady can do bad all by herself. She can get a job and support herself and she does not need to get married to the first "Sugar Daddy" to come along for a short cut. Parents, older siblings and various relatives should not be telling them what to do, like in the play, "A Raisin In The Sun."

America is the "Great Satan" to a lot of Muslim nations because we keep harping against teen marriages. Most normal girls want to get married and have children. There is a story in the Bible about a young lady who was unlucky at love. She was passed down through the family of her "in laws" from one brother after the other who kept dying after having sex with her. I am not sure of her age, perhaps she was in her teens or near 20. However, her father-in-law promised her that when the baby boy came of age he would marry her to him. Very likely the age she was waiting for him to turn was not 18, very likely the age she was waiting for him to turn was 13. She was on a mission. When the father did not give her the youngest son once he came of age, she disguised herself and sat outside by the road and tricked her father-in-law into a one night stand. When the rumor of her pregnancy went all over the hood, she showed proof to her father-in-law that he was the "baby daddy." It's in Genesis, 38: 1-30. This was her purpose in life and life is so short.

Why do we keep putting off love at the highest points of our interest in and need for human affection? Education should not be ripping off our lives. Most of us are not going to profit from the human sacrifices that we are making in shunning love and marriage. World Government, Federal Government or State Laws should not decide for 13 year olds if they are ready for adulthood. They should have that choice and they should have that right to decide their own fate or future. They will know if they want to get married and their decisions should be respected. What if they are trying to choose a childhood friend who is already a friend of the family and whose family members are good people in the community? Their parents can work as life coaches and be valuable to their children's social development. The current public high school system breaks up the family and makes the parents unimportant to their children. Parents can play a role in guiding the young couple towards a successful engagement period with good chaperoning that will build trust and establish a long-term friendship. Parents can help them avoid the pitfalls of isolating and over sexiness in the marriage.

If they fall in love with a full grown adult out of the blue, who is not an obvious pedophile, who is getting hurt here? If this is a good person with an income and good reputation, approved by the parents, what is the problem? Of course 13 year olds should not be walking the streets looking for love, that can get them killed because perfect strangers are very risky. Parents should have a part in choosing a good match for their son or daughter, if they want to get married for moral reasons and to carry on the family bloodline. Another thing, bloodline. Being fruitful and multiplying is mocked by this new modern America. Bloodline means very little in this materialistic society.

Molested children tend towards having sexual needs and desires that intensify with each passing year after 13. They tend toward jumping into sexual relationships under that age of 18. So what is the point of these age limit laws when they are only creating an underground of immoral behavior? Teen marriages can survive attending college or joining the military, if parents would just be supportive. Abortion choice and adoption options create new problems worse than the problems you think it solves. Sexual obsession from constantly dating distracts young people from pursuing their dreams and staying focused. Marriage will make sex a normal part of a teenager's daily life so he or she can focus. They can pursue education towards a career and have peace with God. I know that there are a few states that agree with me, for that fact I am thankful.

A flippant attitude towards sexual fidelity because of all the dating and playing the field will not go over well with a lover who is serious about faithfulness and commitment. The attitude that if it doesn't work out we can always get a divorce will likely mean you will get a lot of divorces. Symptoms of sexual neediness are: chronic dating life, one night stands, using prostitutes for those needs, partly because someone said you were too young to get married the first time you fell in love. Another possible cause is the daily studying that chronic education brings, so that whatever you think about, you will do it. Forced learning takes away free will. You create a passive personality that will follow the slightest suggestion, always seeking a reward.

CHAPTER NINE

BI-RACIAL MARRIAGE

"Then Miriam and Aaron spoke against Moses because of the Ethiopian woman whom he had married...Miriam became leprous..." Numbers 12:1-15

The way our culture is designed, delaying adulthood by five years encourages Bi-Racial marriages. The Silver Lining to this is that Bi-Racial marriages are good for the Black race because every child born from interracial unions is considered Black, no matter how White, Native American, Latino or Asian that child may look. Personally, I would like Black people who look another race to be free to claim that race without any backlash. But in this century, Black people need all the support they can get. As long as love is the priority, not trying to be trendy or "in" with some kind of mixed-marriage club.

Our national co-ed high school system facilitates sexual experimentation hook ups. It is also a strong influence towards Bi-Racial marriages after graduation or in college. Getting married into someone's bloodline should be more about character than skin color. It would be wrong to split up kids only because of different races. It is not the skin color that decides how good someone will treat your child, but by the age of 18 this will be a set opinion in that teenager's mind.

Usually a color fetish happens because of an early bad experience with their own race. It might have been a childhood sex abuse experience, groping, molesting, abandonment or rejection. Or it could have been a rape in which the victim associates skin color with the sexual predator. All children need to be protected from inappropriate touching. Some rape victims seek a protector and get into fatal attractions out of desperation. These victims can become violent and manipulative in their desperation for someone to love them. They have low self-esteem, and they need professional counseling. In a society full of promiscuity most of the attitude is that it does not matter about getting raped or molested because the child victims will get over it. Just suck it up and time will heal those wounds, just get over it. Some judges give very light sentences to rapists and child molesters.

Trying to stay a child in a grown-up world, results in more girls and women being raped and molested at higher rates and statistics every decade. The poor places, with large majorities of Black people, tend to have a large population of convicted Black pedophile rapists. High school has so much idle time no challenges or need to apply oneself, reviewing eighth-grade level classes, and socializing for someone to have sex with. It is such a waste of time. Even if a girl is a lesbian she knows the way to have children is to get married to a man, preferably a cute little bisexual man. Race mixing and lesbianism usually occur after too many bad sexual experiences with your own race, or one great big traumatic experience (like a gang rape).

Unless there is an attraction at a preteen age, most Black girls do not go out of their race to find love. I myself wanted to maintain a type of blind loyalty to Black men, even though Black men never did anything for my well-being. I grew up in a hood where I was regularly stalked, or threatened with rape, so often that it became normal to me. I was one of the ugly girls in middle-school. A lot of Caucasian women are marrying Black men that Black women do not even want. Black teen girls have become so caught up in survival and overcoming poverty that they are slower to accept marriage proposals. They are going to college, delaying marriage, and turning down a Black man's wedding proposals. It is obvious they have missed their God-given moment to fall in love with a sincere and compatible young Black man. Teen aged Black girls who grow up in a poverty zone can become disillusioned with Black men at a very early age and see marriage to a Black man as dangerous and enslaving. If the non-attraction between Black men and Black women continues and increases, within another hundred years American Black people will be replaced by African immigrants. The descendants of America's slaves will be substantially blended into the Caucasian population.

Black men also might have traumatic nonsexual experiences, such as a mother who beat him and yelled at him for every little thing. Poverty is its own worst enemy. It is hard to be sweet and positive with a rent payment coming due, and not enough money in a paycheck to cover all of that rent for the second month in a row. Or when the father is in prison doing hard time for armed robbery because he lost his minimum wage job and bills still needed to be paid. So the son sees this stressed out Black mother and believes in his heart that this is a skin pigment tendency that he wants no part of. A 13 year old could be persuaded to forgive his mother and to go ahead and marry a girl his own skin color, but after 18 that boy will be hating Black women, calling them curse words, too far gone to change.

Once a Black teenager decides to never let go even though he or she is not even close to being relationship material, they tend to play the race card and cry racism when Caucasian parents are taking a long hard look at character. Maybe it would help to make sure the attraction a Black teen has for a non-black teen is not based upon unresolved issues with people of one's own skin color. That child might attempt suicide to manipulate the situation, or threaten murder if denied access to this teen of a different skin color. They see in movies that Caucasians are heroic and giving, so they choose to pursue a Caucasian man or woman for that forever after relationship. Right now in the news there are serious issues that involve the perfect stranger of another skin color that your son or daughter met at school (or on the internet) with hormones raging out of control. Sometimes it works out that good kids of another color come into the family tree. But how tragic when a color fetish turns deadly.

My junior year of high school, I myself resisted the charms of a young Caucasian man, a 6 foot quarterback with gray-blue eyes, dark blonde hair and a Cherokee profile. There were Caucasian girls who hated me for fighting the feeling. I was lusting after every attractive Caucasian boy I met my junior year of high school. My erotic imagination was filled up with daydreams of marrying this or that young man who did not even see me, because they had been taught not to look at girls of other races. The mysterious indifference towards me really made them more desirable than Black men.

I have seen with my own two eyes how a desirable genius of a young Black man lusted so strongly upon the classic beauty of a young Italian girl with long curly reddish brown hair, a perfect coke bottle figure, with lightly tanned skin and sapphire blue eyes and the girl only had eyes for him. I never saw myself as compatible with that young Black man, I pretty much saw him like a brother figure. Well, I should have been Mrs. Right, but he married that beautiful, auburn-haired Italian girl, last I heard. He became a prosperous musician as well. I suspected my father would not approve a Bi-Racial marriage, so I turned down a couple of chances to go steady out of my race.

On the other hand, had I simply stayed home from high school that year, I would not have laid eyes on handsome Caucasian teenaged men in the first place. I was so close to refusing to go, but my own inner desire to make other people happy, even though I knew I would not stay a virgin. I went against my better judgment because I never did anything against the flow before. I never spoke my own mind before, I never expressed my own real ideas or feelings before. I was still trying to be a child. I knew I would fail to measure up to all the adults hopes and expectations that I would not get pregnant and need an abortion. I failed them, but I really failed myself, I should have refused to go to high school until I felt I could survive high school. I was terrified, and the rape threats came at a Catholic high school my sophomore year. I did not need a life like that. The government should be held responsible, but it gets away with it. The rape threat came after a sex education class, such timing.

My younger brother dropped out his freshman year. He was terribly teased by the girls in the hood, they called him a homosexual. He married a Mexican American woman that he met at work when he was 21 years old. She was his first love connection and they are still together 40 years later.

CHAPTER TEN

TEEN EMPLOYEES

"For the love of money is the root of all evil: which while some ear-nestly sought after, they have erred from the faith, and pierced themselves through with arrows of many sorrows." 1 Timothy 6:10

They are capable of learning how to drive, shoot a hunting rifle, hack a computer program or babysit for 8 hours, but they are not capable of working at Jack-n-the-Box? We are training teens to do nothing. Then they look to their parents their whole entire lives until their parents are too old to keep taking them in and bailing them out of their messes. Sure a few do well, a few get lucky, but the vast majority keep losing jobs because their upbringing never trained them to persevere through difficulty.

We have made life too complicated for our own good. We are overly concerned about education's role in getting a job with benefits and a pension. The problem with that is, opportunity to make it rich can arrive on the scene at 13 and disappear at 18. Especially for young people who are gifted at sports, art, music, writing, dancing, acting, modeling, public speaking and journalism. Love can arrive on the scene at 13 and disappear at 18. We keep wanting a magic number to call adulthood. Adulthood is not a number; adulthood is the ability to clean your house, get your body out of the bed on time to go to a daily job, and say "no" to crime with no one watching over you, plain and simple.

Many poor neighborhoods have high crime rates due to young people trying to make money at 13 years old. Giving them the right to work full time, after 8th grade graduation could help drive down the crime in the poor neighborhoods. I cannot guarantee any of my theories. We no longer display the 10 Commandments in our public schools, we no longer pledge allegiance to the flag and join the ROTC programs, so I cannot guarantee that the future emancipated generation will be moral and righteous.

I do know that not all poor people are criminals. There are poor people who have pride in keeping the 10 Commandments; who have faith in God out of a true conviction to keep God's commandments; and who would not resort to violence or stealing to pay their bills, all out of respect for God. We need to instill in our children that not all money is good money. They need to be proud about what they choose to do with their lives. Not all people are cut from the same cloth.

A prostitute mother does not always intend to raise up a prostitute daughter. Let young people choose their own path when you are done raising them after 13 years. Parents need a way out and so do their teenagers. If 13 became an emancipated age in which one could live on one's own and get a job without being labeled a delinquent, that would be a step in the right direction. It is not all about sex because some teens have homosexual developmental disabilities or no interest in sexual relationships, just Platonic friendships.

Emancipation is more about freedom from mom and dad telling them what to do all the time. There is the right to leave home and find a private resting place and visit the parents once in a while. Freedom means a lot to all adults. Children don't normally want or desire the absence of mom and dad, but young adults do. Our country is behind the scratch ball when it comes to our replacements. We seem to have no intention of letting our children take over our jobs. We do not believe in apprenticeships when they turn 18. We help them pack for college or the military. We erase so much of family legacy, pride and history, all because of education.

We let them leave the farm with blessings. We gave birth to them hoping they would keep the farm going. Then we stopped our teenagers from working the farm at age 13 and made them feel stupid for caring. So now they do not care about the farm. They want to leave as soon as they turn 18 and never come back, not even for Thanksgiving dinner. When the parents pass away, the farm will go into foreclosure. A farmer's son or daughter can go to college and become a politician, movie star, rap singer, or astronaut; while mom and dad run the farm all alone with arthritis and aches and pains. No sense of loyalty or family ties. We all want a lawyer, doctor, bank manager, professional athlete or performing arts star in the family; but the family business, a legitimate career, should always come first. A job is survival: no job, no survival. College is only part of a dream job: an immoral background, lack of social skills, selfishness and such like will count against getting and keeping that dream job.

Adulthood at age 13 will help poor girls get the respect they need from men. As they work hard on their jobs to support their younger siblings at home, staying off the streets and keeping to themselves. They will grow into hardworking women who know how to solve problems in a legal and sane manner. They will not likely be welfare recipients. They will probably become business women who own employment agencies, daycare centers, beauty salons, restaurants, private schools, churches or dollar stores. The early confidence gained from early legalized adulthood or emancipation will be priceless towards changing the face of poverty. A 13 year old with a clean demeanor, still a virgin and sweet and innocent, could work his or her way up in a fast food restaurant and become a manager by the time he or she turns 18.

Most fast food restaurant managers make 40 to 50 thousand dollars a year starting pay. A lot of college graduates who grew up poor would be happy for that kind of salary. If only America would stop this compulsive homophobic sexualization of our heterosexual girls and just let them dress sexually neutral and save themselves for marriage. It would help towards respect on the job. Most hookers have been raped or molested in their childhoods. A little girl has no clue that men are attracted to her or that little boys are turned on at seeing her thighs or belly button. Stop pushing college education on poor kids, not every poor kid is meant to have a rags to riches story. Make the American Dream all about keeping a job once you get one. Too many young people are quitting jobs because they want more money instead of living on a budget. Not being a quitter is the best possible job stability and work history. The friends you make from staying on a job most of your life can prove priceless. The American Dream needs to be clarified so that young people will stop job hopping and failing to thrive where they are planted. It is just as much the American Dream to have a regular job that supports your basic needs through living on a budget and being happy with what you make. Being a loyal employee and making friends on your job should also be part of the American Dream. College debt that exceeds the amount of money you make in one year on your regular job is counter-productive towards living the American Dream.

Give 13 year olds legal rights to begin living on their own, to go out and get a legitimate job; not drug dealing, not prostitution, not shoplifting like the present day. I am referring to legal rights to move away from an abusive situation in the home. How can any-one be expected to attend high school with a major crisis going on in the home? Yet that is what goes on all the time in our society. The public school system keeps casting blind eyes to the home problems of students who are literally raising themselves. They should not have such a stronghold on a child's life that the demands of the school system matters more than the problems of the child. When you work you get constructive criticism, you get given direct orders, not suggestions, you do things you do not feel like doing at that moment, where is the public school preparation for it?

We have raised up about two generations of pampered and entitled groups of poor people who seem to be going from bad to worse. They expect their parents to work themselves into an early grave while they go to college for career choices they do not have a chance of working in. They sit around their parent's house and refuse to do any kind of housework. Most of them live inside a "dream" and lose their sense of "reality". Their Dream Careers require morally strong and unselfish employees. There is no type of curriculum that gives that to young people. Maybe church school, but church school is not normally taken seriously. Even church kids follow lock-step to the government. They do not save themselves for marriage, they do not work outside the home to help with the rent, they are just as messed up and lost as everybody else. Another thing, living within their means, putting money away in a savings account, as though they are buying a car or paying on a mortgage.

We keep raising Dreamers who have no sense of reality where their income and salary are concerned. They begin at the age of 18, the age parents are done with them and they are done with their parents, if they are lucky. However they have not acquired any skills whatsoever at living within their means. This hurts them for longevity in a job choice or career. They keep disrupting their homes and moving back in with mom and dad because of living one paycheck away from homelessness. Or they simply fail to thrive. If they had begun the process at 13, their chances of survival and success at living on their own would be greatly increased. With their parents supporting them, they could be taught about the cost of living in an apartment or a house. The amount of income it takes to live comfortably on a minimum wage salary or a collegian's salary. When the child is 13 the parents could teach them the value of staying out of debt by showing them how debt will decrease their financial freedom. The parents could also show them the value of keeping a job and retiring from that job if it has retirement benefits. The 18 year old has no interest in any further communication from his or her parents, just packs and leaves.

Dr. James Breakwell makes a profound statement concerning training children to one day work a job, in his book titled, *BARE MINIMUM PARENTING* he writes: *"…you mainly want your kid to pay their own bills and not hit you up for money every month. At some point, the freeloading has to stop. It's just a shame it doesn't end earlier. Good luck getting grocery money from a toddler. When it comes to your child's future job, the money matters, because if they don't make any, that money will come from you."*

CHAPTER ELEVEN

TEEN IN CHURCH

"My son, hear the instructions of your father and forsake not the laws of your mother." Proverbs 1:8

All children need a God to fear doing wrong and all children need God and a religion of some kind to mature properly. Believing in a higher power gives children faith in something supernatural outside of mother, father and themselves. When life becomes unpleasant they can pray to that higher power for strength to endure the hardness. Someone to pray to helps them through the hard times and guards their minds against irrational responses to events out of their control. Irrational responses like going to a school and shooting everyone that hurt their feelings or committing suicide over negative FACEBOOK.COM comments. American teens are expected to remain children from age 13 to 18, which goes against nature and God's will for most of their lives. Bible thumpers quote "Be fruitful and multiply" and "God said it is not good for a man to be alone," but they do not see that it applies to all humanity, including their under 18 children. Is high school necessary for success at life? We need to stop feeding our children lies. We keep telling our children that it's okay for them to be able-bodied and never lift a finger to lighten their parents' financial burdens—that is soul destroying and a sin. Children are our replacements. We will not keep working much longer past the age of 50.

It is time to stop discouraging and ruining young lives with these age limit laws. There are great minds, gifted young 13 year olds in our world today. We need to give them a chance at adulthood. There are so many more advantages in the 21st Century than they had in 1900, but that does not mean drive your beautiful virgin teen to the Bunny Ranch in Nevada. Do you understand what Jesus was talking about in the book of Mark, chapter 7, verse 11, when He said, It (education) is corban (a sacred gift)? Which made the commandment to care for the parents null and void. The most ambitious people on the planet are in a church of some kind. "Honey no, you just worry about graduating from high school" "Idleness is the devil's workshop" and "corban" is a sin. CORBAN is refusing to financially support your parents because you are too busy getting an education. Plenty parents grow to resent doing all the work outside the home when their children have not lifted a finger to help them inside the home, homes in America should be pristine during those high school years.

Let children pray about their lives. Let children decide the direction the school curriculum is taking their lives. Let children have the right to say "No more educational institutions, thank you very much." The USA is long overdue to stop victimizing the children of America's poor. They still walk around uneducated and disenfranchised because of the false promises of a very flawed, immoral, and godless educational system. Let God be the head of household again. Let God decide the avenue of a child's learning curriculum. Let God decide if a child is ready to quit school, get married, move out, get a job, etc. A system that is parasitical, enslaving and torturous to the souls of massive numbers of young Americans, guarantees failure to thrive after high school. We support a system that encourages selfishness, hatred of authority and a fear of commitment or leading a natural and normal life. It makes marriage, love and family look like failure and limitation; and singleness with college debt looks like a life to boast about. Fatherlessness is encouraged and commitment is frowned upon, but the human soul was not designed for this inhumane makeover.

Even without being a prostitute, there is still the shame of having more than a couple of sexual relationships outside of marriage. Who wants a woman leader with a reputation of immoral behavior, like a lady minister for example? Or who had a couple of abortions? Or who married more than once after a divorce? Can she run for President of the United States? Christian parents have been passively going along with these traditions of men as though God ordained this ferocious, myopic obsession for material gain. What is wrong with loyalty to your family? What is wrong with helping your parents? As long as it isn't a sin, what is wrong with parents training their children to work a family business at the age of 13? If only Christians would take a stand and let their children be different from the children of the unbelieving world. Seeing the stronger marriages and family ties would cause the unbelieving world to follow the lead of the church. It could also evangelize people when they realize how important Christian faith and keeping Commandments of love is to a happy marriage and family.

Courting should always be chaperoned because talking is the goal. Money and a car is not necessary when two young people are strongly drawn to each other and it is not a light "puppy love" or a passing attraction. Once again, not all children will require tough love. Get them emancipated anyway. All children are smarter than we will ever understand. We cannot preach morality and lock them in their rooms to keep them pure and innocent. Would it have worked on us? Then let us stop wasting time and breath and do what is moral in the sight of Almighty God. We need to honor our children, stop provoking them to wrath and take their needs SERIOUSLY, even their need to be free from parental domination.

The meat and potatoes of being a human being is denied to this generation and those to come. They are not allowed to be human beings until they turn 18 and by the age of 18 their lives are messed up beyond all repair. Girls and boys who were virgins at 13 start sleeping around with everybody and anybody since their parents say they are too young to get married. There is anger and rage in their hearts for their own moral failure. There is depression behind abortions and sneaking around to have sex behind their parent's back. They did not take those attractions seriously in those early years because they were told that they are too young.

The "idol god" called "college" is the ultimate goal at all costs. It is not love, family, having children and living like a normal, God-chasing human being. They have been forced the first 13 years of their lives to chase financial success through education: not through serving God and living according to the Bible. Insanity is doing the same thing over and over again expecting it will be better this time. When will we stop the insanity. When will we give our children, regardless of gender, gender orientation, race or immigrant status, the right to a life while going to public school? The public school system should adapt itself to the needs of the children, not the other way around. On the contrary, the church is trying so hard to be friends with the world that the moral values of their children suffer. They shut down a natural first-love attraction with a girl or boy in their church, they abort a teen pregnancy in secrecy, and some of the teens trying to live holy and remain virgins are despised and accused of being Gay or Lesbian. Nature calls at 13, the church knows that, God is not about a legal age law, God puts urges in our bodies. We want to work jobs, we want to get married, we want to raise children. The church should be pushing the government to change child labor policies to accommodate God in their lives.

Teen church girls in America can do better than their sisters in 3rd World nations who are forced into arranged marriages. We have rights and laws already in place for their protection. Teens who don't want to get into any trouble with the law are suffering as I am writing this letter: this idea is for those kids. In America there are "Good" kids who are smart enough to take on responsibility. They put on an act and submit to their guardians, parents and teachers because of age limit laws. They put on a fake smile and stop trying to make decisions or figure out solutions to problems because of a legal age law that prohibits them from taking care of themselves. They are legally obligated to suppress their egos another five years before they can oppose their parents' rules and live openly according to their own personal needs and passions. There are books and parenting laws that stop parents from encouraging their 13ers to grow up and take care of themselves. So who gets the right to emancipation? That is very tricky. Mostly a child actor or performer who is making millions of dollars. That is not fair. There are 13ers taking care of themselves in the poorest neighborhoods. They have earned and deserve emancipation also.

People will arrange weddings for dogs but our culture objects to teen marriages, how backwards and wicked is that. Here is the era of calling Good evil and Evil good. Do not trust them on Sunday evening in some kid's bedroom for hours at a time while the adults eat and watch TV in the living room. Without adult supervision for hours at a time, they are having sex. Are you dumber than a doornail or just pretending? They are having sex. Soon as you walk into the room everybody gets in their corner, then when you leave they hop back to it. I repeat, sex is not a sin. You make it a sin. Stop hindering teens from pairing off and getting engaged to plan a wedding and a future for themselves. Being fruitful and multiplying did not have to be spoken twice to the 13ers of The Holy Bible. Women's liberation should not be the destruction of morality.

Teen girls can be liberated and still live holy. They no longer need to go to extremes and act like robots. There will never be a perfect wife, mother, father, or husband. We can only do our best and be the best person we can be, that is the glory of God's Grace and Mercy. Where are the religious leaders calling this legal age policy a straight up sin! Are they so comfortable with the world that they have fallen asleep concerning God's legal age policy? I am a witness to how church folks will separate a girl from a boy she just had a baby with. If churches don't come correct, people will stop believing they are for real and will stay home and worship God in their own way. I strongly believe it is time for the United States of America to allow 13 year olds to assume full responsibility for their lives and destinies.

Also, early adulthood will help religious 13 year olds who get caught doing what their parents warned them not to do. The extremeness of the strict fundamentalist church parents can frustrate teenagers and cause them to become angry at God and anything remotely religious. Fathers, please, calm down and think of the future and keep your family together. Look at your budget and see if there is money for a small kitchenette apartment. Plan a wedding before you even speak to them. You know, your teen and his or her closest friend?

A 13 year old might need to defy a parent or two in order to live by the Words of the Holy Bible. High school is not in the Bible. Birth control and Promiscuity Dances are not in the Bible. Nor is keeping your sons and daughters babies until age 18. There are no good teenagers, just teenagers who cooperate. We are only human beings, not angels from Heaven. The children are our future only if we release them to make their own decisions and choose their own paths. It is happening all the time in our society, but it is not God's doing, it is our society's doing from the decades of mandatorily attending these government run facilities. The myth that "college education" is the key to success is crippling and soul destroying. We can stay home and educate ourselves, there are no obstacles to a quality education in this age of computers and the daily mail. It takes good character to keep a job, good people skills, ability to work with others and putting your own needs to the side.

Where in high-school do those values get taught? Yet parents go along with these traditions of men as though God ordained this ferocious myopic obsession for material gain. We have buildings full of school teachers imposing their values and usurping a parent's authority. It was only a luxury and a convenience. Our church kids are losing faith in their own ability to make decisions and to believe in what the Bible says about sexuality. This is because Christian parents are submitting to age limit laws that state that their 13ers are not capable of self-control, job training, driving, sustaining a marriage, or raising children. There is no such thing as a "good teenager" just teenagers who are cooperative.

Even allegedly "good" teens will betray their parents' trust because they are profoundly lonely and desperate for love. Also, because childhood is ending and natural desires to be fruitful and multiply are taking control like a "human mating season."

CHAPTER TWELVE

MULTI-MEDIA AND WARDROBE

"Now she had on a coat of many colors, for the king's virgin daughters wore such apparel..." 2 Samuel 13:18

I could not say "Finished" without reminding parents of what they already know. They already know that television, radio, music, movies, videogames, sports and social media impact the quality of life for a vast majority of America's teens. Multi-media has an impact that can inspire and heal the hurts of a lonely teenager. On the flip side, multi-media can kill a lonely teenager. In her book, *RAISE YOUR KIDS TO SUCCEED*, writer Chris Palmer writes nine pages of expert advise in chapter 11, CONTROL AND LIMIT SCREEN TIME. She begins by telling parents unshakable facts about media influence upon their teenagers' lives. *"Media and technology have become a powerful second family to children exerting a significant influence over their emotional, social and mental development...."* Parents input, supervision and approval or guidance is still needed with every use of social media and its different forms. The worse thing a good and caring parent can do is "trust". Make sure to the best of your knowledge your child is not being bullied or seduced through social media and internet websites. Some young people who have made a career of sneaking around when their parents go to work, likely will look for love on the internet.

This a clean and non-narcotic outlet to escape the drudgery of forced learning. They are also encouraged to find love, even though their biological clocks just woke up. God, Satan, angels, demons and mortal human beings like celebrities, movie stars and pop-singers all become part of a teenager's fantasy life. A fantasy fife helps teens get their minds off of problems in school and in their own homes. All teenagers need to be in a relationship with someone who thinks the world of them. They tire of instruction and correction, all they hope for is a relationship where they are seen as equal, not inferior, pretty and perfect, not needing to be fixed. A fantasy becomes necessary when love is a dream. When childhood is needlessly dragged out another five years with no hope of finding love in the real world. Then when a girl does meet a boy, he is usually extremely critical and interested in sex. He wants to change her into a sexier person than she is. Parents need to pay attention to drastic changes in wardrobe and self-image. A young adult might not be able to articulate why he or she is acting out. Parents, this is why I have written this book. It is better to work with this human being towards an efficient transition into adulthood.

It is a losing situation to coerce and manipulate a teen, as I have seen on the Dr. Phil show. This teen might begin to become the perfect child you want out of pure exhaustion with your lack of understanding. Once this child turns 18, he or she will pack those bags and disappear, usually with a boy or girlfriend helping with the suitcases. Or all alone, joining the military or going on to college. They will not forget how tyrannical and insensitive their parents were. Very likely, this teenager acted out to deal with depression. Without a real life friend to give a positive affirmation of his or her image, this teen created him or herself into this sassy and defiant young adult who does not care what anyone thinks. That would have been a clear cry for help, help to transition into an adult role and to prepare for adult responsibility. A fantasy life can be a healthy response to helplessness of being forced to attend co-ed public school and being forced to sit on the couch while mom and dad do all the work. When the teen starts trying to make fantasy into reality that will be a real problem in which teachers and parents must intervene. I do not agree with a total lack of acceptance, I agree with acceptance.

If your son or daughter is drinking and having sex by their own choice do not look shocked and call Dr. Phil. Look at the possibility of guiding this child's lifestyle choices so that he or she can keep the socializing from interfering with making a living, attending school and other responsibilities. If they want to smoke, drink, cuss, be promiscuous or dress like a hooker, then counsel them calmly and rationally. There is a time and place for all those activities and people who are age appropriate for doing those things with. You may not approve, you may not be ready, but the best response is to go with it, not against it.

It is not the end of the world if you raised a person you do not like. Be careful with that sense of mature superiority. God-given gifts can help a child survive a rough life. Even the Bible says "A gift will make room for you." Mocking a love of music, singing, dance, acting or sports is just like picking a fight with a pit-bull. Do not make an enemy of your child because of what is not in your control. The government is already controlling your life kindergarten to 18 years old. The movies they watch, social media friendships, video games and music taste will have an influence on young adults, the goal is that it will help through the dark days.

Once again, parental supervision might be needed if a strong drop in joy is obvious. Do not deceive yourself, rap music/heavy metal occasionally, not daily. Like pain pills, too much anger music can he hazardous to your health. Eight hours a day of "ZENA THE WARRIOR PRINCESS" and "S.W.A.T." can also stimulate violent behavior and the desire to shoot guns. Another violent movie based upon a videogame is "Alita, Battle Angel." If you want a more aggressive 13er; show them these films on purpose.

Harry Potter, Avatar, Hunger Games and the Twilight Trilogy impact not only teens, but young people in their twenties who still are acting like teens. A few grown-up people are drawn to these stories because of a childhood that had a dominating school curriculum. Perfectly attending a government controlled curriculum which deprived them freedom of choice, has a lifelong negative impact on many Americans. These movies portray courage through impossible odds, winning a fight and outlasting the bad guys and true love that is dependable, caring and protective which blossomed from innocent friendship, not the consumer mentality of dating.

[WARDROBE] This generation has so little that they can count on, so many human rights put on hold or completely denied in hope of achieving some kind of imaginary success that they cleave to colors and attire that portray their strongest interests. Be concerned about black, it always means negativity and poor self esteem. Be concerned about sexually provocative attire. Sometimes girls and boys go into denial, after all they do not have emancipation to think of themselves as adults, while trying to stay children to get along with their parents, their clothes betray them. Take action and help these teens meet good people who you want in your family tree, do not leave it up to lust and random chance. A perfect stranger can be a danger. Do the background check. The emptiness of forced education and worry about the future make clothes, and colors, a way of making friends, of belonging and of course, of getting attention. It helps them survive, but it also helps them cry for help.

CHAPTER THIRTEEN

THE "TOO YOUNG" EXCUSE

"Seven years old was Jehoash when he began to reign."
2 Kings 11:21

You can shoot a rifle and kill your first deer at 5 years old, drive an ATV or ride a pony, but you better not try to quit high school, get a job, get married and move into your own home at the age of 13 years old. You mean to tell me that it is okay to teach children excuses for not working a legitimate job that they can excel at? It is difficult to go from being a baby to being an adult in a one year period. It makes more sense to work at adulthood for a period of years before the age of majority. Even without being a legal age, viewing 13 differently than we do right now, would help young people be more mature by the age of 18. There will always be excuses for keeping our sons and daughters at home and away from strangers.

We are in a society now that born again believers do not take it seriously when their daughter gets pregnant out of wedlock. The abortion clinic is full of Christian teen girls covering up their sin of fornication. To what end? We are coddling and pampering and over-instructing and over-parenting our children so much that they do not trust their own judgment. They do not pursue their own dreams, they do not follow their own heart and soulful ambitions. They sit and wait, usually in front of a television, for their parents to tell them what to do.

They will always be too young to live on their own, to control their own destiny, to make their own life defining decisions. At 13 years old childhood is a choice for a vast majority of America's adolescents. Most of them are fully developed mentally and psychologically, in spite of the original reason for legislating age limits to adulthood. Being told you are not old enough to do something is very harmful to a teenager. God could be calling that boy or girl to impact society by going to college, getting a full time job or getting married and raising children. This delaying of adult responsibility could be interfering with a call of God upon a young person's life towards a positive destiny. It is like our government expects God to cooperate with their age limit laws. What makes 18 so special anyway? Divorce is guaranteed to happen after the age of 18 by 50%. Wendy Williams (TV talk-show hostess) has a philosophy of life that a young lady should date around before settling down to one man for the rest of her life. Wendy said that 23 was too young to settle down and that she reluctantly got married in her late twenties, so maybe 30 is the ideal age for marriage in this century, the new sweet 16. The over-parenting would likely arrest the young people's emotional development to such a degree that the age of 30 makes sense for taking on marriage and child rearing.

Am I the only person in America who sees this as appalling? How is it a good thing to stay a child in a modern nation, up to the age of 30? How does this make any kind of sense? We need to trust the judgment of 30 year olds. We need 30 year old police officers, lawyers, judges, teachers, social workers and priests to be fully grown up and fully mature. We need our 30 year olds to have experienced marriage and child rearing, not to still be single hoping to mingle. Not to still he wearing bobby socks and chewing gum and chasing every cute person they meet. Is that not what we have today? Nothing matures a person like a covenant marriage and being good at raising children. Even longterm employment does not grow a person up like marriage and family life Also, the high moral code of marrying in virginity. Marry for love and no other reason. When you see someone cuter remind yourself of how much you have gone through with the one you are married to.

We are hurting our country, and possibly the world, with these laws that tell an individual 13 year old you cannot work a full time job, sign a lease and live by yourself. Hey, smart, mature 13 year olds cannot get married without a parent's consent, give birth to their own children and raise up those children in their own home, paid for by their own legally hard earned money in the United States of America, but they can in Asia, Africa and Arabia. In the USA, when a 13 year old has a baby it goes to adoption. If he or she had sex with an adult, the adult goes to jail, no matter that it was mutual consent. They cannot legally run away from an abusive parent or leave school and work a job to help their parents pay the bills. I am not interested in forcing my ideas on all of America's young people, but this adulthood at 18 has been forced on America's young people far too long, like some kind of an experiment where the scientist has died and people are suffering and no one is trying to stop this runaway train.

Our country is falling apart with the collateral damage of obsessive prolonging of childhood with the co-ed public High-School system and its "Junk Food" education. I hope and pray that enough people will see my point of view that it will become an issue to be voted upon. This "status quo" educational system facilitates rape, sex traffic, abortions, drug abuse and promiscuity. It contributes to a welfare nation and an entitlement mentality when you stop a 13 year old from going out and getting a job. No one needs to do research or read a book, just look at the difference in our young people when they graduate from 8th grade and how much they change by High School graduation.

Of course they still need their parents pouring philosophy into them. They will also need to do what adults do: build up their muscles, take martial arts and boxing classes, purchase mace, harmful toy guns, pocket knives, etc. to be strong and prepared. They will need to mind their own business and not be easy to make friends with cute people, because cute kids are often the biggest con artists. Freed from the forced socializing of high schools today, tomorrow's 13 year old adults will have a greater chance of avoiding bad company that corrupts good manners. America will never be a great nation again without taking charge of the young people and addressing what will make them better as people. It is very difficult to parent someone who is torn between readiness for adulthood and laws that prohibit adult responsibilities. Today's 13 year olds are keeping their focus upon pleasing parents and teachers and not pleasing themselves.

They have no other choice but to watch hours of TV and eat snacks that make them fat. By default they often grow up to become alcoholics and drug addicts. It is crippling to a human being to extend childhood beyond 13 years old and mandate excessive schooling practices and excessive years of submissiveness and inequality to the authority figures in their lives. This encourages rebellion and hatred of authority. In the middle of this, suicide and murder are encouraged. Not all families are running smoothly with moral boundaries and compassion for academic failure. We hear stories more and more often of parents locking their daughters in a bedroom to stop her from running away with a perfect stranger. The problem is not the pedophile in this case, the problem is that her parents ignored her need for love and romance. There is a natural and normal process of becoming a woman.

The Mormon faith has very bad press about men who forcibly raped 12 year old girls and have a polygamy culture. It is probably simple sex traffic disguised as religion. The Mormon faith that I know has a very good culture in which their sons and daughters make friends with people of their own age group within their own faith and upbringing. They support virginity and allow their teens to marry and give them lots of support within their community. Thirteen year old girls are easy prey to any male who pays them attention. Parents need to pay attention, because the strangers "girls" fall in love with become a part of the family tree. I also advocate hyphenated last names so that the young person does not lose his or her identity through marriage, or get mistaken as a blood relative of a family she or he has married into. I think the married name should replace the middle name in cases where the hyphen is against someone's religious beliefs.

If parents would just pay attention and do something about their lonely young teens there would be fewer horror stories to put on TV. Horror stories not only about runaway teen girls, but also about boyfriends murdering the teen girl's parents who had the nerve to try and tell her she could not be with this man. It is becoming too common to see teen girls marrying bad older men who treat them like slaves and beat the soul out of them. Parents can curtail all of this by acknowledging that 13 is an age of change. Parents need to address their daughter's and son's need for love. They need to do their job, they need to find a suitable match, a compatible young person that they will approve of for their family tree. Parents who cannot see anyone being matched with their son or daughter are selfish and foolish. Let those children go and they will love you, hold them tightly and they will hate you.

For your own good find your child a compatible boy or girlfriend. With 13 as an age of adulthood or emancipation, parents should take it upon themselves to arrange a good marriage choice for their sons and daughters, instead of the present custom of leaving it up to "Random Chance": no child brides, that is a losing game. Teens must marry for love and equal physical desire towards each other, period. Virginity on the wedding day needs to be the goal.

There is no way to stop people from arranging "Child Bride" marriages, I am sorry I have no solutions to that issue, but I hope that awareness will help people to see that it is wrong to force a teenager to marry someone too old and too mature to enjoy being married to an adolescent. Thirteen and eighteen can do well together growing into maturity and experiencing life together, but thirteen and twenty-one is going up to the line where it will be like a bossy parent all the time. Once the honeymoon is over, the more mature one will fall into a parent mode. How in the world could that be a happy and fulfilling marriage? There is supposed to be equality in marriage, not a parent-child relationship from beginning to end.

The willingness of the teen is what is most important, the teen must want to marry this person, and parents are doing well to look for a good match, healthy and attractive, that the thirteen year old would be happy to get engaged to. Also, there is a real good chance, because of lust, that this marriage will not last until they die of old age, but virginity should always be lost in a romantic and committed setting. So the first marriage can be the "virgin marriage" if 13 became the emancipation age. Virginity is a good thing and a gift to your husband or wife on your wedding night, it also creates a spiritual bond. Sex is so delicate and personal, that losing virginity in the back seat of a car, at a party or through a drug induced stupor will bring more shame than joy. Marriage is the best hope for a virgin teenager to turn out well from a first time sexual experience.

Wikipedia: The Free Encyclopedia, states the following about Childhood: *…the age span ranging from birth to adolescence. According to Piaget's Theory Of Cognitive Development, childhood consists of two stages: Pre-operational Stage and Concrete Operational Stage. In developmental Psychology, childhood is divided up into the Developmental Stages of Toddler-hood (Learning To Walk), Early Childhood (Play Age), Middle Childhood (School Age), and Adolescence (Puberty Through Post Puberty). Various childhood factors could affect a person's Attitude Formation. The concept of childhood emerged during the 176 and 186 centuries, particularly through the educational theories of the philosopher John Locke and the growth of books for and about children. Previous to this point, children were often seen as incomplete versions of adults. The term "childhood" is nonspecific and can imply a varying range of years in human development. Developmentally and Biologically, it refers to the period between Infancy and Adulthood. In common terms, childhood is considered to start from birth. Some* *consider childhood as a concept of play and innocence which ends at adolescence. In the legal systems of many countries, there is an Age Of Majority when childhood officially ends and a person legally becomes an adult. The age ranges anywhere from 15 to 21, with 18 being the most common...*"

We need to stop caring what other countries are doing. If 18 is working in France, Germany and England, good for them, but it is not working for America. It never has worked for America, our moral well-being has been declining since the child labor laws first stopped 13 year olds from working full time jobs and getting married. "WE'RE TOO YOUNG!" seems to be a chronic mantra for people who do not want to change their lives.

"Too young" needs to stop being an excuse. The average 18 year-old should be assertive and confident in his or her readiness to handle adult responsibilities, but they are not ready. Starting at age 13 to prepare for adulthood makes good common sense. Adulthood means living alone and keeping yourself out of trouble with the law. You must be 100% consistent with arriving on time to a job. They must make payments on schedule on a car, rent and utilities. They must live on a monthly budget and stick with it. They must speak their minds with calmness and control, when feeling upset, instead of resorting to violence and shouting. That will not happen in the blink of an eye as soon as someone turns 18.

CHAPTER FOURTEEN

PERSONAL STRUGGLE

"Train up a child in the way he (or she) should go." Proverbs 22:6

There's no Biblical precedent for putting children in public schools and forcing them to learn like drones. Refusing to work and contribute to the family is a sin. From the moment a child says "Ba Ba", "Ma Ma" and "Da Da" education should begin. It should also end before childhood is over. Children should have a one year break to rest from education and reconnect with their families. From personal experience I would make 13 the age for emancipation. Once again, I am not trying to destroy a parent's place in a child's life. I would like to see a "Christian values" upbringing emerge in our society regarding decisions to get married before having sex, and putting off high school and college to help the parents with bills and rent, also a Christian value. I want very much to see and meet a new generation of moral successes and happy adults.

Once again, I am not trying to demean a parent's place in a child's life, I am desiring to expose and uncover an alternative for the more delicate young adults in our society who feel pressured to act out with aggressive behavior, narcissism and immorality. Not trying to use the Bible to prove my point, all I really need is personal experience, observation and the feeling in my gut that someone needs to speak up for all the 13 year old young adults in this country. At age 18, I still needed help with a lot of stuff because I was no smarter than when I was age 13. I could not hold down jobs or relationships because of my strong spirit of competition, and it still plagues me in my 60's. Knowing I have a personality disorder does not help me when I do not even know what "normal" is like. I was lucky to have a mom who gave me a lot of "me time." She had simple rules, just do what she says.

She did not chronically critique me, she left some things for God to change. I went to school on an empty stomach, with 4 hours of sleep from studying and doing homework. I had not had any time with my family, school work was a priority. My mom was the sole source of income, no child support, no welfare money. She barely could afford our rent on LPN student and housekeeper pay. Our clothes were often gifts from her friends. My brother suffered the most. He wore the same pair of shoes to school from 6th grade to high school. He dropped out of school his freshman year of high school because he could not handle the ridicule. The system does nothing to help. If the system wants to invade our homes, then it should pay us for our cooperation. We should be getting paid for good behavior and making grades above average.

Most of my best friends in the 8th grade were juvenile delinquents. They were the boys and girls who were sexually active. They smoked, drank, cursed and resorted to bullying to solve their problems. They were very intimidating. Some of them worked odd jobs and drove their own cars. Most juvenile delinquents are victims of abuse or over-parenting. A 13 year old juvenile delinquent couldn't care less what the law says and will do as she or he pleases. One young man got married at 13. No one could tell him to have babies out of wedlock and let his father keep taking care of him. I am very proud of him as I was back then. He did okay with his life. Much better than I did. I despised those A's on my report card because they never put food on the table or shoes on my brother's feet. I could not get what the big deal was to the children of college grads.

I studied until midnight and got up at 4:00am to do homework in the future chapters, from the age of 6. This was my response to being laughed at. No one would ever again call me dumb or a copycat. In 8th grade I witnessed a teacher making passes at the handsomest boy in the school. She was 30 something and chain smoked. It made me angry at her. I felt robbed because I adored him and he never ever knew it. He died at 30 years old of cancer and he did not smoke, nor did his parents, I wonder how he got that cancer so young? Don't get me started on all the male teachers who chased after the most beautiful 8th grade girls in the Roosevelt School District. I am not a snitch, so I won't be naming any names, but this is why I am writing this book.

These were not innocent little girls. They were not claiming to be virgins. A couple of those girls claimed to be "Head Hunters" as young as when they were in the fourth grade. A certain light brown skinned young lady with a broken arm, used to yell in the breezeway her name and how her blank sure wasn't sorry. You call that an innocent little girl? If I were her parent, I would rejoice in knowing I could put her out of my home and in her own apartment once she turned 13, as long as I give her financial support until she gets a job and make myself available to her for protection and supervision.

Sorry, but you need to know what a mixed bag of nuts poverty brings. Some children are perfectly raised and some children are the offspring of prostitutes, pimps, drug dealers and child molesters and do not know any better. By 8th grade graduation I was exhausted, I did not look forward to high school. I imploded in high school. I changed my name and pretended I was my own cousin, like 'Patty Duke". I never competed to be the smartest again and I still graduated in the top 5%. Why? What was the point? In elementary school I was commanded to learn things I will never ever use or see again.

I acted out once I turned 15. I could not hold back any longer. My natural hormones were fighting against my religious belief in marriage before sex, but I did not realize that I would one day regret not fighting for my human rights. I needed love and I did not fight for love, now I am all alone in the world facing eternity as I approach 62 years-old. I have taught myself not to think about it and to focus on the bad side of having someone in my life. When I found a young man at the library who was everything I could ever want in a husband, my mom rejected him. She also threatened him with jail time if he ever spoke to me again. He was the one for me, rights to marry would have given me permission to disobey her.

I tried to move on, I kept going to church, I kept doing well in school, but I could not keep going indefinitely, and I snapped after about six months. I made a scheme to lose my virginity to another virgin and then stop the relationship after finding out what all the drama was about. Just one time was what I thought we agreed to, but he had a hidden agenda. I planned on returning to church and repenting for fornication and living in celibacy until another chance for marriage came along. My scheme fell apart when the young man became a sex addict. He could not quit the relationship when I was done with it. I felt betrayed and confused. He got something out of sex that I did not, but his mother called me an opportunist and a bad influence. Secretly I wanted to involve the adults, but I was afraid for the mental state of the young man. I did not want to marry him for real, but I considered us spiritually married to deal with this forbidden sex life. Now I was just another moral failure in the Black community and no longer a role model.

We used our right to abortion because I needed to cover this mess up. I had never done anything in my life this stupid and dumb. I felt humiliated and forsaken by God. How could I ever go back to First New Life? How could I ever face Sister Golden or Mother Sledge again? If only I had been more scheming when I worked summer jobs and for Jack-n-The-Box. I would have socked away all the money that I made, but instead I spent all the money that I made for clothes and food. Age 18 seemed like an eternity into the future and I did not see the future. I lived for the present. I could have made plans to move into my own place, but I was not sure I would live to see 18.

I knew kids who had been murdered. I felt endangered the entire four years of dealing with the problem of Co-Ed Public high school attendance. I was under the impression that it would ruin my life if I refused to attend high-school while I was not mentally ready to attend. It ruined my life attending high-school. I was threatened with rape at Saint Mary's High School; and I was threatened with rumors of a race riot at East High School, so I never planned on seeing 18 years old. I was supposed to succeed based upon my good grades and good behavior, but I began adulthood right at 18. I had opportunities to assert myself, but I failed to take a stand. I thought it would hurt my mother's feelings if I told her what was in my best interest. My mother knew I was unhappy, but she could not figure out what was my problem. High school, for me, was a waste of time, and I deeply did not wish to attend high school. I got nothing out of high school. At Saint Mary's I made one true friend whom I turned against because of racist peer pressure.

I tried to attend four high schools so I could be the new girl every school year, but I stayed another year at Saint Mary's to please my mom, so I attended 3 different high schools. Being the new girl helped me have privacy. I still believe I would have had a better life if I had just stayed home from high school, worked at Jack-n-the-Box and entered community college with an 8th grade diploma at the age of 15. My 7th and 8th grade courses were equivalent to a freshman college curriculum and the three high schools I attended never came close. I looked like a woman at 13 years old and there I was still being raised.

I wish my mom had arranged for me to get married and start my own family and my own life. She might have were it not for this cursed legal age law.

I remember being mocked by a HUNDRED OF MY PEERS FOR BEING A VIRGIN, during summer school in the cafeteria. The boy said, "Would all the virgins please leave", and everybody looked at me. I guess a boyfriend I bench-pressed off of my belly must have told everybody my clean little secret. I watched over my two younger siblings like I was their mother. I cooked sometimes, I cleaned the floors, I washed the dishes and sometimes I bossed them into helping me. I never said in my mind, "I am too young to do this." It would have shocked me to find out that divorce and poverty put me in that position and that there were children with mothers who stayed at home doing all the cooking and cleaning for their children.

I have faint memories of when we lived with my father, no affection and we hardly ever talked. My parents were nobodies to me before my mom left my dad. We three children were always at home doing nothing all day waiting for my daddy to get home from work. My mother watched a lot of soap operas and talked to her girlfriends about getting a job to have her own money. We would play outside until it got dark. We were isolated from other people, no relatives and no other children were involved in our lives. Our mother was an abuse survivor and very protective of us. Going to kindergarten/church were just dreams.

I am articulating what so many cannot put into words. When I was at the young age of thirteen I could not enunciate what I was feeling. I never spoke my own words, I lived inside my head and I was afraid of being ridiculed and seen as strange or stupid. I knew given the opportunity, I could govern myself as good as any adult. At the age of 60 I feel like I have no one to impress. While I live and breathe I feel commissioned by Almighty God to put out a book addressing this issue. I believe there are people who do not feel this is important. They had a great childhood and they loved co-ed public high school and being controlled by successful parents every step of their lives and their lives are happy and prosperous this very minute because of all that.

I hated violence as a child. I never felt like a winner for beating up a boy for groping me, contrarily, I felt like a loser. I made up my mind at 13 that sex is not for kids. 1 chose to fight against boys and men who wanted to have sex with me. It made me hyper vigilant and paranoid. I refused to give in to sexual desire no matter how badly I wanted to be with a handsome young man. Forty-seven years later I am a hundred percent sure that I rejected my God ordained heterosexual match.

If thirteen had been the legal age back then, I would have married the only young man I ever really loved. I would be a grandmother and a wife in a 46 year old marriage. Because I was trans-gender and lived like a boy for 4 years, I was physically and mentally prepped to defend myself against the 7 year old child molesters and rapists among those innocent little baby faces. I never reported Elbert and Willy, because I had been taught not to be a tattle-tale. I fought my own battles against those sexually aroused little freaks, now full grown men. I wore shorts under my dresses, no one had to tell me. It would have been nice to have school uniforms covering my thighs and calves, hey, a pantsuit, what a novel idea. Not allowed in that school district—dresses, skirts and culottes, above the knees.

If I had considered myself having the right to refuse to go to high-school, to take control of my life, I could have testified to a HETEROSEXUAL CHRISTIAN CHURCH that I was born with Transgender and Lesbian tendencies and grew out of that when I fell in love with my husband at the age of 13. Kids like I was, who didn't want to get into any trouble with the law suffered the guilt of having secret sex lives outside of marriage at 13. This letter is for those kids: Good kids who were smart enough to take on adult responsibility but who submitted to their guardians, parents and teachers because the law said they must suffer another five years before they can oppose their parents' rules and live openly according to their own personal needs and passions.

I want frightened young people to have a legal right to stay at home from the violence of a crime infested neighborhood. I also would like young people who choose to go to school to get on with a college education and also to have a place to escape a criminal and violent home life through legal rights to run away from home and the rights to live on their own and act like responsible/mature adults. I also would like those young people who are more sexual than others to have the right to get married and live like adults, instead of hiding and sneaking around. Why should they live in shame? God made them virile for a reason, fertility is a gift, not something to be belittled by society and suppressed by standing up for the Kingdom of God's moral values. Government mandates. People should marry off their 13 year olds as a religious right, standing up for the Kingdom of God's moral values and giving their child a real life worth the trouble of getting up everyday.

I did all I could do with Elementary School. I was burned out from all the work that I put into being the smartest kid in school. If I had the legal choice, I would have stayed home until I felt courageous enough to deal with the roughness of public high school. We are all different. I hated high school, people thought I was being cute, an 'A' student hating high school seemed like a joke. No I do not have a Master's Degree in Child Psychology, I have a Master's Degree in the College of Hard Knocks. I was a child left home alone after school from age 6 to age 17.

I believe the age of thirteen is a maximum age for childhood's end and a minimum age for adulthood's beginning. I struggled with going to public High School. I was the valedictorian, student body President, 10th of the Top 10 State Spelling Bee Champions of 1970, the chronic over-achiever wherever words needed to be memorized, defined or spelled.

Blaming no one but myself, I did not have the courage or the self love to take control of my life. I waited for permission to sell my short stories and poems and the permission never came. Probably because there was no money in the house to publish books and poetry. So that part of my life that could have supported me did not bear any fruit. Had I the prerogative to think of myself as an adult, I would have kept a summer job and worked it full time. I would have published my books and poetry and lightened my mother's financial burden of feeding, clothing and sheltering three pampered, healthy, entitled, highly intelligent, obedient and respectful adult-sized children.

CHAPTER FIFTEEN

DEAR PARENTS

"...but as for me and my house, we will serve the Lord."
Joshua 24:15

No other government in the universe should take control of teenage lives like this one does. I am not grateful that I did not have the right to live on my own and make my own decisions for my life at the age of 13. Was I the only one who felt tired? Was I the only one who needed a vacation from education? I am aware of The State of Virginia's effort to help 14 year olds who get pregnant by giving them the right to get married. Virginia had this backwards. 13 year olds should be given adulthood, the same as if they were 18. Of course, they should not be marrying people old enough to be their parents, but if a person over 13 wants to marry a 13er, that person should be counseled to make sure this is love. It would be no different than legal age at 18, except it would all happen sooner. Parents would have a better child to deal with, minus the baggage of high-school abuse.

I was reading about Roe v. Wade and the article declared that birth control pills were originally invented for Black People, to keep down their numbers. It worked, and it is still working. The most damaged race of people have bought into this evil practice; hook, line and anchor. It has been a self imposed genocide all along. Adulthood at 13 would have saved and prospered Black People by now. I am referring to poor Black People, the stereotype that most Americans think of, the matriarchy, the crime zones that people try not to drive through after dark. The children they refer to as the "Cream of the

"

Crop" push aside their natural affections and desires to control themselves from falling in love.

Then they fall into immorality before the age of 18 because there is no place to run and hide from sexual temptation. How ironic that the Black athletes could have done something by now to make sure every Black child has the advantages to become law abiding citizens. They are not givers, because they were not taught to give. They were taught to be selfish and self absorbed in their teens, an abnormal way to raise up young men. Their loving, indulgent mothers probably did not even bother them about taking out the trash and doing household chores. Still speaking of Black Athletes and why they consistently show a lack of concern or compassion for their childhood friends and communities. Not allowing them to be fathers in their teens, not enforcing a code of conduct that they better choose a life mate and not a temporary helper, has negatively impacted their personalities as full grown men.

Speaking of poor Black People, Black Athletes should be standing in the gap. The saddest part of all is that since they were never trained to help their families they do nothing for the poor. They were never trained to care in their teens, when it would have made a difference in their manhood. They were not allowed to be men in their teens, but now people expect them to suddenly care about others now that they have earned millions playing a game for a living. Still speaking of negative stereotypes concerning the poor Black People of America. A horrible majority have been taught a bunch of new norms. (1) Do not fall in love. (2) Do not father a child you created. (3) Do not quit school and work a legal job to help mom pay the bills. (4) Put all adult responsibilities on hold until the age of 18 or college graduation. Not just the athletes, but most young Black Men who grew up poor and put off adulthood until age 18.

Poor Black People cannot afford the show tickets, yet the celebrities do not reach out to help the "Housing Projects" that they grew up in. They have no philosophy to share, no insights to a successful lifestyle and they do nothing to end crime and poverty in the ghetto. They just keep on ignoring the Elephant in the corner while they sign an autograph or two, visit a sick child in the hospital for a photo op, but no one gets a dollar of their hard earned money for free. They keep chasing after a "rainbow in the sky" with their college loans, abortions and living single. Then one day they realize that all that "pot of gold" chasing was a big mistake. By then they are just too cynical and sour on life to fall in love and raise babies.

Marriage forces a boy to become a man. When a boy becomes a man from raising sons and daughters, and from forging a strong relationship with the partner of his virginity, dealing with the peaks and valleys of keeping a job and living on a budget. he can become fearless, as well as fulfilled. America is moving into an era where the real courage will come from inmates. Men who have survived the prison culture will have the confidence to join the military and go fight a war. Even the Boy Scouts of America has announced that they will be integrating with the Girl Scouts. We will need to recruit juvenile delinquents to replace our aging soldiers and police officers if we aren't already doing so. A matriarchy is being created by a society in which fathers do not matter. There are aspects of manhood that women cannot relate to and will never bring up in the course of a young man's life. It takes a father to challenge a young man to see how strong or brave he is. This is a "momma's boy millineum." They simply do not respond to macho authority figures.

There will be fewer soldiers, masculine leaders and male warriors coming out of the public school sector. Young women will step up to the plate to take on jobs that fewer American males will seek after. These young men will direct their masculine instincts into selfish pursuits instead. Without the confidence to be a manly man, most of America's young men will avoid traditional male occupations. I also heard on the news that Arizona legal age laws will allow 15 year olds to get married, but they need parental consent. So who is it going to help? This will still encourage a "child bride" state. I do not understand why parents are so afraid of their teens choosing marriage, over sleeping around.

There are some children who have very low IQ's, but they will still get lonely. Help those children embrace virginity by focusing upon a job, or vocational training. Meeting people and making friends at church, work or school can usually sustain special needs children. Maybe God Our Creator has placed autistic children in this world to show us how bad it is to treat children like robots. Even though they can survive without sex, they will still need space, not all that nagging and being treated like a slave.

Take them out of public high-school with its bully culture. Give them an open forum to vent and discuss the abuse they suffered, but most importantly, do not buy a gun for them. Karate lessons are a lot easier to pay for and will build their confidence. If they are happy staying home, give them a small apartment set-up in their bedroom or a basement bedroom with a mini-kitchen and a bathroom and a back door to go in and out without your watchful eyes.

Treating all fourteen year-olds like adults will boost their overall sense of well-being and lift them above "suicidal depression."

Most children dream of love, the perfect job, a beautiful car, losing weight and becoming more popular. They might not find love in their teens if they have disabilities, but as they become more mature, without being bullied everyday and told they are losers everyday, they can grow in confidence and bring someone to meet mom and dad in their later teens or early twenties. I would be more afraid of my under aged teen having sex outside of marriage. In a dirty place, or a public place without love, or by force not consent, or with the help of alcohol or pills. Then what if the teen falls in love with a person who was only seeking a one time sexual experience? There are so many wrong ways to lose virginity and be scarred for life. I wrote this book because it bothers me that America's teenagers are not allowed to obey God in directing their own lives and that is just wrong, or to put it another way, it is a sin.

I do not believe in forcing people to be children who feel they are ready to live as adults. That is why I believe 13, not 15, is the age to fight for. Please open your eyes and see. Open your ears and hear. Then stop getting angry and upset. Your child is old enough to have a baby and your child is having sex or making decisions to lose virginity with a certain boy or girl on a certain day after a certain birthday or on that day or about 10 days before that day. Some of the really smart ones have been having sex since the sixth grade right under your noses. Wake up parents, for the love of God, please, please, open up your eyes and your ears to the sound and the picture of your child's sex life at 13 years old.

Sex is the most natural and normal drug that almighty God has put in a human being's DNA. Gay or straight, your child is old enough to mate. If your child is 13 years old, your child is no longer a child. The sweet innocence is gone. Train them while they are young or you will not get this chance again. *"A child left alone brings its parents to an open shame."* Forbidding and controlling will only work to destroy your relationship with your child forever. Do what will work to keep your family together and to meet your teen halfway. Once a week have a family meeting and allow that teen to voice his or her wants, needs and complaints without people getting upset or telling them to shut up. God deals with teenagers and a teenager might become a juvenile delinquent or "ratched" due to disobeying the call on his or her life. Or the opposite, the teen might become a doormat, easily controlled by every bossy friend. This is the result of over parenting. Most of this generation has this problem. Some teenagers medicate themselves with drugs and alcohol while others get hyper religious and use God as an excuse for saying "NO" to drugs, alcohol and sex.

We are guilty of doing too much for our young people. We need to let them grow and we need to let them go at the age of 13, even if they do not say that they are ready. Like the bald eagle kicks its young out of the nest, that is what we need to be doing with these over grown human babies. Give them a place to live, teach them how to drive a car, help them get a job, and let them supervise themselves. Mom and Dad, driving is a very serious and important skill to have, it is also dangerous. Teens need to learn the rules of the road before the age of 18. Knowing how to drive at 13 is a survival skill. Unless the middle school has a driver's education course. It is important to teach what is of interest to your child before the walls go up.

When our culture had "shotgun weddings" there were probably some failures but there were also successes. We like to throw out the baby with the bath water in this nation. Let us get a grip and mix an old value with some good common sense. We need our youngest teens to grow up and take on human responsibilities. We need to stop raising our children to be losers at love. Let us stop preparing them for lives of moral failure, prostitution, gang banging, drug dealing and addictions. This government controlled culture specializes in creating adults who become drug addicts to dull memories of abortions, rapes, incests, molestings and personal anger and hatred. "DADA" is written in the DNA of most babies as they say that word before any other.

When teenagers come up pregnant we will be doing our jobs to wed these young people together immediately so a child will be legally fathered. What they do after that is really their own business, but my expectation is that they will do their best to make it work. We cannot step inside their skin and make them be good parents or a loving couple, but we better do like our grandparents once did for us, because we are a dying breed. We had self esteem from being born in wedlock. Every child in the world should have that gift. Do not keep depriving your own future bloodline of a tradition of marrying the father of the baby that your teen girl will soon be giving birth to out of God given attraction, whether you approve or not. Marry those teenagers off when they fall in love. Get them jobs and their own homes, cars if they know how to drive, and put them into a community college, rather than deal with the silliness of high school any longer, or the dangers of a University campus lifestyle.

We can right a wrong and give God back his authority over our children's lives. We have held them too close for too many generations and all we have to show for it is crazy people. While they are believing in love, we can guide them into moral choices that will place them in God's hands. Back in those days the Bible was the main book that was studied. They said the pledge of allegiance and the Lord's Prayer at the beginning of the school day. We did not ignore the spirits and souls of children like we do today. Parents, we are not naturally immoral, contrary to popular beliefs, left to ourselves, we will marry for love and have babies in wedlock.

This is a law that a true believer in Jesus Christ had better break in order to have a clean lifestyle and a clean conscience before God. A Christian 13 year old must find a job, or two part time jobs to help with the bills and the rent when there is only one adult as head of household. That is being a hero, a giver, a Good Samaritan, a follower of Jesus Christ. Do not encourage them to date before they are ready to mate. Dating always gets out of control. There is no way being alone with someone you are lusting after is a good thing to do. Better to be accused of being gay, than create a baby before they are prepared for the responsibility of child rearing.

We turn up our noses at the idea of teenagers getting married and making new relatives. We thoughtlessly give away the children that the teenagers created by mistake, not design, into the foster care and adoption system. So we have already created a new normal that involves "not getting married to the one you loved when you were a virgin, and giving away your flesh and blood newborn babies like it's no big deal." We are forcing them to go underground with their sex lives. We are forcing them to lie to our faces, to steal our money and whore themselves. We force them to forge documents and pretend that they are 18 when they run away from home.

We force them to have haphazard sex in the back seat of a car in the middle of a field in the dark like sex is a sin. Sex is not a sin. Babies are not a sin. Have we stopped behaving like a Christian nation? Have we become Lovers of pleasures more than Lovers of God? Twelve months can fly by, it might take a teen twelve months to make one adult decision, but at least they got started. Thirteen is a perfect starting point. Adulthood needs a beginning and there are twelve year-olds having sex and babies, but they are still children in their minds, no doubt about that. A 13 year old can look like a baby in the face but come up with all kinds of wisdom and common sense, that is how I know that this is the age to fight for (adulthood.)

Why are the men so angry in the last days? Why is there so much unnatural affection in the last days with bad behaviors and rabid acts of selfishness? Age control might be a reason why. Forced learning with no profit or benefit to the family, might be another reason. At an age they should be raising babies with baby talk and kid TV, they are fornicating like wild animals and watching hours of violence from morning to night until they are old enough, by rule of law, to leave home and get a job. Jobs help you stop watching so much TV. Raising children helps you watch less violence on TV.

Here is a balance that has been lost for the past 50 years or more, and its impact is rising. We won't have a choice, the fruit of this evil regime will create men so fierce and dangerous at such early ages that we will need to lock up all the guns and sell them to professional gun carriers only. The way back is to change the game and rules of engagement for 13 year-olds. Reward them for good behavior by allowing them to open up and tell you what they really want to do with their lives, then you, as parent and protector, help them attain that dream, as long as it is not a crime.

They will still need lots of guidance, but the purpose will no longer be the ungodly purpose of keeping them down and holding them back. God will bless parents who seriously guide their children towards adult responsibilities. When they work a job while living with their parents, they should always give a portion of their checks to their parents out of respect. If you read this with a right heart, you will read between the lines that I care deeply about children, who will grow up to be adults. I want America to stop holding children down, stop ignoring their intelligence and their potential to educate themselves beyond and better than a public school curriculum.

Also, the moral code of children, to want marriage instead of shacking up or sexual experimentation. The original command from God was "Be fruitful and multiply" this is a consuming urge of (every) normal 13 year old. Why can't parents help them find an awesome match? What is wrong with love? Love should not be a bad or forbidden thing. I could have been matched to an awesome young man in my church who went to college and never married. Adult society is too carried away with education.

Here is the generation that blesses women who have never had a child. Here is the generation where virginity is despised and virgins become promiscuous in order to fit in. Here is the generation that forbids marriage, that dishonors parents, blood, heritage, legacy, Family Crests, extended family and family businesses. Here is the generation of disfigurement to fit an imaginary model of beauty, skin burning, skin bleaching, wigs, weaves, baldness, vain enhancements, tattoos and skin painting, but what about the babies? Who is raising the babies? Who is being the stay at home mom? Who is normal or at least old fashioned enough to raise the next generation?

So it is really ironic how this responsibility so often falls upon the Grandparents. We need basically good people, not extremists, not fanatics, just kind-hearted, naturally patient, unhurried, hard-working people with low sex drive or no sex drive, to raise our children in the USA. God's model of two parents, one staying at home while the other earns the paycheck for food, shelter, clothes, toys and transportation is still relevant today. We have already created a new normal that forbids working for money as soon as you are physically and mentally able. The government tells you when to get married, when to get a job, when to have a baby, buy a house, learn how to drive, etc....

We have already created a new normal in which people in the Land of the Free do not make their own decisions and choose to follow their own path when they are finished with being parented and behaving like a child. Also a new normal of law enforced childhood by rule of law. Over protecting, over parenting, over indulging and over pampering children who have what it takes to take care of themselves. They are not allowed to behave in a normal way towards the opposite sex, so they become immoral and deceitful behind their parents' backs until their 18th birthday. Then they come out in the open or run away from home. Some will never write or call again.

We are over parenting, no wonder they have no confidence in making their own decisions for their lives. We are making them impotent with all our fears of the future. They do not all need college to become middle class or rich or successful at life. Age control is not a rich kid problem, or upper middle class, but those who are struggling financially need to have their teens working jobs that will not put them in jail. The government knows this, but will do nothing about it.

Five years is a prison term, but the government tells 13ers they cannot live their lives as they desire. They must attend a mandatory Hell Hole, known as high school, while their parents or parent struggle with keeping a job and roof over their heads. In cases of today, parents might very well be homeless and jobless. The culture believes for the 13er that a high school diploma in five years will save them from the problems that they are having in the here and now. What will save the day is that a fresh faced, pure hearted virgin gets a job flipping burgers or busing tables, cleaning floors or washing dishes. What will help that family is the freedom to post-pone high school until family problems have been cleared up. What will help that family is the freedom to use an 8th grade diploma to get into a community college and take CLEP exams.

With millions of poor children attending public schools our country is backwards. People are more illiterate and more criminal than they have been since before high-school was invented. We have made an idol out of education. You cannot talk five minutes without someone talking about high school or college. So you have a bachelor's degree in something important but what is missing? A conversation about a virgin son or daughter getting married and wearing white on their wedding day. A conversation about helping their teen find a house, drive a car and buy baby clothes. The Idol God of Education has replaced the stability of following our hearts and our own natural bend. We are expected to go without sex another 5 years, crippling our natural and normal ability to be strongly attracted to the opposite gender. The unnaturalness of dating teaches unfaithfulness to one person. High school is a waste of time for so many young people, just a glorified babysitting service.

Why does our society want to keep teenagers babies? They are failing miserably at trying to be what they are not. By rule of law we put them in high school and begin to haze them and diminish their egos, to what end? If I am being forced to attend high school against my will, then at least have the decency to treat me with an iota of respect. I don't need to be groped, raped, molested or lusted after, I need to be respected as a grown woman, whether I am 13 or 130 years old. No hate on public school teachers. They deserve a starting salary of $50,000 and a max of $100,000. They are the true co-parents of our children. They are the uncles, aunts, grands and great grands that a lot of these illegitimate children born of illegitimate children do not have in their own family experience.

Teachers deserve all the rewards and all of our admiration and support. Teachers have shown their true loyalty by dying with their students in school shootings. No one should disrespect public school teachers. They are just pawns in this board game, they have very little control, they are caught in the middle. Parents and teachers need to rise up and demand that the government stop dominating the curriculum. Parents and teachers, and their teenagers can come up with a better curriculum that will serve the students, instead of making servants out of the students and stunting their natural development. High school is so backwards and so insane it would not surprise me that when the Baby Boomers are all gone, we will not have this same type of government, because we will reap the fruit of America's public high school system. Cheerleaders, jocks, musicians, dancers, actors and Goths. How does this system create World Leaders for tomorrow? The public school system as it stands right now is really Satan's greatest invention.

You might think you came out okay, but really, did you really? There was a time when a Christian young lady wore clothes to go swimming. Now we are looking the other way and doing nothing about it when our Christian daughters wear pieces of string and 3 triangle patches to go swimming. Teasing men is the norm, no one complains about, better not. Women want respect, they want men to behave like good boys no matter what they do, even when they themselves behave like bad girls.

We do not want young people to get married, sex is not worth your life, even after they have made a baby, so we give them birth control pills. Love is just a feeling that will eventually go away. Where do you think we got that from? We did not get it from the Bible or from a sermon. We got it from attending public school and we did not even feel the sting of the needle.

Once we get it through our thick skulls that 13 years is long enough to be a child, it will get easier to prepare our sons and daughters for adulthood with each new generation. Quoting from Dr. Phil McGraw's bestselling book, *FAMILY FIRST—"Will your children withstand the pressures of their lives and worlds, or crack when the going gets tough? Is theirs a strong foundation for what is to come? The answers to those questions depend largely on how you mold and shape your children, their values, their behavior, their ability to make sound decisions on their own, and how well you honor their individuality and nurture their unique gifts and talents. In short, it depends on what you do today to help them become responsible adults tomorrow...."*

I am moved to tears typing this book. All I really want to do is give more choices to our grown up teenagers. They should not need to become counterfeiters, shop lifters, drug dealers, prostitutes and pimps. They need more room to grow up at the age of 13, more choices to be who God wants them to be and to decide for themselves, with some parental guidance, what direction their lives need to take.

CHAPTER SIXTEEN

THREE POEMS

"Suffer the little children to come to me and forbid them not."
Luke 18:16

I wrote a book on the situation,
There was no hesitation,
I do not care about my reputation,
We need a reality-based education.
Most of the children are having sex,
Most of the children have an "ex"
By the age of 13.
Know what I mean?
This is the time parents lose track,
Innocence is lost that you can't get back.
Most of them are fully grown
And shackled to the telephone.
Most of them don't ask for advice,
Most of them are not very nice.
They are angry and frustrated,
Tired of being dominated.
Give them a chance to make a choice,
Give them a chance to have a voice.
They might not be so mad,
They might not act so bad.

There is a lot of yelling and screaming,
Because who can survive on dreaming?
When do they have a say?
When do they get their day?
You have faith they can wait 5 years,
Then get ready for some tears.
Keep them really close,
On a leash wherever you go.
Lock them in the bedroom,
Let them eat cake to cope with the gloom.
Release them from mandatory schooling,
Mandatory lusting and drooling.
Parents that have control,
Know how to tie up the soul.
Some parents will use violence,
Some parents will use silence.
Some parents will tease them,
A few parents will attempt to please them.
Calling a 13er a child is crazy,
Not helping them to be emancipated is just lazy.
Then giving them 5 years more
Before they can go out that door.
What are you training them to do?
To always live with you?
To hesitate about getting a job?
To sit in a room and become a blob?
To have babies outside of wedded bliss
Through the gateway of a first love kiss?
No plans, always hit and miss,
How backwards in a time like this.
13ers will do what they really don't want to do,
Because of how much they love you.
This is an age God could be calling,
And the hedge of childhood could be falling.
An age of thinking for oneself,
Not believing in anyone else.

An age of testing limitations,
An age of imitation.
Wanting to have fun,
Wanting education to be done.
Wanting to share one's life,
Wanting to be a husband or wife.
Hating authority figures,
Setting off emotional triggers.
Always defying orders and rules,
Feeling like parents and teachers are fools.
Forcing young people to hide their truth,
Despising them in the days of their youth.
They hear what they want to hear,
While their children pretend and fear.
They see what they want to see,
While their children practice hypocrisy.
Not my daughter, not my son, not my child,
But when you leave the house they go wild.
How do you expect them to survive?
How do you expect them to stay alive?
Denied basic rules of being flesh and blood,
Drowning in hormones like a flood,
Fighting for respect with fathers and mothers,
Fighting for privacy with sisters and brothers.
A government conspiracy,
To spread around the misery.
By the rule of law 13ers are not to work fulltime,
No wonder so many of them resort to crime.
Not that it is an excuse for doing wrong,
But people get discouraged in prison too long.
People lose faith in a higher power,
When they are bossed and pushed around every hour.
We have a government that dehumanizes teens,
Doesn't care about your values or your genes.
Doesn't care about your feelings or needs,
Doesn't care about your talents and good deeds.

It sets you up to lose your moral virtue,
High school will always hurt you.
It puts 13ers in a herd like a flock of sheep,
Controls everything about you including how much you sleep.
The ones who wish to please perform the best,
The thinkers refuse to join in with the rest.
High school is a "Hell Hole,"
Graduating early should be the goal.
Depression and backwards morality is the norm,
After four years the "good" teens will conform.
Claim your religious rights and do it God's way,
Help your 13er survive and truly save the day

Sing a song of sorrow
For the future of tomorrow.
Sing a song of regret
For unwanted babies that mothers forget.
Dead now, so they won't be poor,
Dead, dead for sure.
Sing a song of tears,
For the victims of their mother's fears.
Maybe there's a soulless cell,
Not just Heaven or Hell.
The unwanted invader of my womb,
Was set up to experience an ultimate doom.
Because I was Pro-Choice,
This is my body and I have a voice.
Keep abortion legal for women like me,
Always in and out of love and so very unlucky.
Women who get pregnant at the wrong time and place,
Need abortion to make "unwanted ones" disappear without a trace.
Keeping my life uncomplicated was the way I played the game.
I was relieved after an abortion and I didn't feel guilt or blame.
Is this a sin? Did I take a life? Did I kill a baby?
Yes. No. Maybe.
A safe haven, a refuge, should have been my womb,

But for this unwanted baby my body was a tomb.
Then another unwanted baby came along
And I couldn't repeat what felt so wrong.
In the Book of Psalms, 139:13
Saying, "God covered us in our mother's womb," what a scene.
Then in the Book of Jeremiah 1:5,
I got a clue to keep this baby alive.
It said, "Before I formed you in the belly I already knew,
Before you came out of the womb I sanctified you,
And I chose you to be a prophet to the nation."
Which gave me a reason for hesitation.
For that new unwanted baby inside my womb,
I did not volunteer to be a tomb.
I don't know what the future may bring,
But with faith in God I did the normal thing.
The Tomb for the Unwanted Baby is who I used to be,
But I felt so bad about it that I begged God to forgive me.
My mind has changed, no more guilt and shame,
My life will never be the same.
I give respect to my womb,
Never again to make my body a tomb

Poverty was just a word,
Which I so often heard.
It became my jailer,
And labeled me a failure.
I fought and clawed for government assistance,
And got all kinds of contempt and resistance.
With hope, dreams and a gift,
Poverty's fog didn't lift.
With the progress of jousting against the wind,
The path of poverty did not end.
I saved and lived within my means,
I couldn't eat like kings and queens.
I got deeper in debt trying to get ahead,
All my hopes and dreams dropped dead.

I have college debts and no kind of job,
People believe I'm a do-nothing slob.
Poverty is a straight jacket holding me tight,
Everything I do is wrong and I do nothing right.
I should have kept up with Jack-n-The Box,
Excelling in the college of life and hard knocks.
Worldly pride is not God's will for me,
The School of Life gives me a PHD.
Don't jump into colleges cold and blind,
Better have a place to work on your mind.
Don't scorn jobs that don't require school,
Nothing surpasses the Golden Rule.
Are you bragging about yourself,
And wishing you could be someone else?
Do you make others feel sad?
Do you make them angry and mad?
Why should God bless your pursuit?
Are you that sweet and cute?
Poverty does not need to be like prison,
Tell the poor people Christ has risen.
Do not let poverty get inside your soul,
Be poor but happy, that's the richest goal.
Don't let poverty make you cry.
Don't let poverty make you die.
Let God oversee your poverty,
Let God show you what others cannot see.
While in the quicksand of poverty you grow old,
Family and friendships are the true gold.
Set your admiration on things above,
And God will make you rich in love.

Thank you for reading this book.

BIBLIOGRAPHY

Breakwell, James, *BARE MINIMUM PARENTING: The Ultimate Guide to Not Quite Ruining Your Child*, Benbella Books Inc., 10440 N. Central Expressway 800, Dallas, TX 75231, 2018.

Carey, Kevin, *THE END OF COLLEGE—Creating the Future of Learning and the University of Everywhere*, Riverhead Books of Penguin Group, LLC, 375 Hudson St., New York, NY 10014, 2015.

Delisle, Ph.D., James R., *UNDERSTANDING YOUR GIFTED CHILD FROM THE INSIDE OUT: A Guide to the Social and Emotional Lives of Gifted Kids*, Prufrock Press Inc., PO Box 8813, Waco, TX 76714, 2018.

Golus, Carrie, *USA TODAY, LIFELINE BIOGRAPHIES: Tupac Shakur—Hip Hop Idol*, 21st Century Books of Lerner Publishing Group Inc., 241-1" Ave. North, Minneapolis, MN 55401, 2011.

HOLY BIBLE-KING JAMES VERSION, Vision Street Publishing LLC, 1575 N. Park Drive 101, Weston FL 33326, U.S.A.

Koestler, Ruben and Marina, *HOW TO TUTOR YOUR OWN CHILD*, Ten Speed Press, Crown Publishing Group and Random House Inc., New York, 2011.

McGraw, Dr. Phillip C., *FAMILY FIRST: Four Step By Step Plan For Creating a Phenomenal Family*, Free Press of Simon and Schuster Inc., 1230 Ave. of the Americas, New York, NY 10020, 2004.

Palmer, Chris, *RAISE YOUR KIDS TO SUCCEED: What Every Parent Should Know*, Roman & Littlefield Pub. Group Inc., 4501 Forbes Blvd. 200, Lanham, MD 20706, 2017.

Peacock, Nola, *HONOURING OUR KIDS: How To Encourage Growing Hearts & Minds*, Advantage Media Group Inc., Charleston, SC 2016.

Schermund, Elizabeth, editor, *CAMPUS SEXUAL VIOLENCE: AMERICAN POLITICS*, "At Issue" series, Greenhaven Publishing LLC, 353-3rd Ave. 255, New York, NY 10010, 2017.

Young-Bruehl, Elisabeth, *CHILDISM: CONFRONTING PREJUDICE AGAINST CHILDREN*, Yale University Press, New Haven and London, England UK and Grand Rapids, MI USA, 2012.